FREE Study Skills D\

Dear Customer,

Thank you for your purchase from Mometrix.

As a way of showing our appreciation and to help us better serve you, we have developed a Study Skills DVD that we would like to give you for <u>FREE</u>. **This DVD covers our "best practices" for studying for your exam, from using our study materials to preparing for the day of the test.**

All that we ask is that you email us your feedback that would describe your experience so far with our product. Good, bad or indifferent, we want to know what you think!

To get your **FREE Study Skills DVD**, email <u>freedvd@mometrix.com</u> with "MY DVD" in the subject line and the following information in the body of the email:

    a.   The name of the product you purchased.

    b.   Your product rating on a scale of 1–5, with 5 being the highest rating.

    c.   Your feedback. It can be long, short, or anything in-between, just your impressions and experience so far with our product. Good feedback might include how our study material met your needs and will highlight features of the product that you found helpful.

    d.   Your full name and shipping address where you would like us to send your free DVD.

If you have any questions or concerns, please don't hesitate to contact me directly.

Thanks again!

Sincerely,
Jay Willis
Vice President
<u>jay.willis@mometrix.com</u>
1-800-673-8175

LSAT®

Prep Book Study Guide

QUICK STUDY & Practice Test Questions

for the Law School Admissions Council's (LSAC) Law School Admission Test

Adapted from LSAT Secrets

Published by

Mometrix Test Preparation

LSAT Prep Books Team

TABLE OF CONTENTS

Success Strategies

This guide provides a series of helpful test-preparedness and test-taking strategies to prepare for any test. Implementing these strategies will maximize your chance for achieving your goals on test day. However, there is no trick or tip that can replace the importance of studying over an extended period of time. You must have a firm grasp of the material. Consider your favorite sports team. Do they just show up on game days? Of course not! They meticulously practice every scenario and prepare for a specific opponent. You should bring the same focus, dedication, and hard work to prepare for *your* opponent—the exam.

Studying Strategies

1. Become intimately familiar with the instructions and format of the exam. This includes knowing the time allotted, number of sections, and number of questions per section.

2. Develop a long-term study strategy. Remember, the most effective learning occurs over an extended period of time. Your brain needs adequate time and space to process new information. If possible, start planning and studying more than a month in advance of the test.

3. Set a goal. This is the first step in creating an effective study strategy. What do you hope to achieve? Is there a minimum score you must meet? Taking a practice test before studying might help you develop a baseline.

4. Create a stable study environment. You should establish a consistent time and place to study. Select a place that is quiet with few distractions and allot enough time to sufficiently focus on the task at hand. Treat studying like an important appointment and stick to a consistent routine.

5. Prioritize organization during your studies. Consider using a single notebook with a matching folder. Also, keep study tools like pens, pencils, highlighters, sticky notes, and tabs conveniently located near your notebook. Write down your goal and schedule, and keep this information with your materials, perhaps on the first page of your notebook.

6. Study the comprehensive review. This study guide includes goes over the important content for each section. Read this information, highlight important parts, and make notes in the margins. Create flashcards for new terms or concepts and review them often.

7. Answer practice questions. This is one of the best ways to study. This guide includes practice questions, and these practice questions mirror what you will encounter on the big day.

8. Review the answer explanations. All practice questions in this guide have corresponding answer explanations. Whenever you get a question wrong, it's important to know why the answer choice you chose is incorrect. It can also be helpful to read the answer explanations for the questions you got right. This helps you remember the information and better understand why it is the correct answer.

Final Preparedness Strategies

1. Spend the afternoon and evening before the test doing something relaxing. Since you have developed and executed an effective study plan, you must accept that you have done all you can to prepare for the test. Cramming will not lead to any meaningful improvement, and it could lead to confusion and increased stress. The downside vastly outweighs any potential benefit. Treat yourself to a relaxing activity to put your mind at ease. Go to a matinee movie, take a walk in the park, finish the book on your bedside table, or anything else that will get your mind off the test. After all that studying, you have certainly earned some rest and relaxation!

2. Prepare your test materials and snack before going to bed the night before. The test instructions you have reviewed will describe what materials, if any, are required for the exam. Preparing these materials in advance will avoid an unnecessary and panicked search on the morning of the test. In addition, if there is a break during the test, prepare a light snack to ward off distracting hunger pangs. Try to pack a protein bar, granola, trail mix, or a handful of tree nuts. Lastly, take note of any prohibited items, like cell phones, and make sure you do not bring any into the test site. Possessing a prohibited item is often grounds for disqualification.

3. Develop a plan for arriving at the test center. The night before the test, verify the location of the test center. Whether you're driving or taking public transportation, make sure you are familiar with the best route. If you're unfamiliar with the area, look up traffic patterns or common delays at the time of the test. Also, make plans for backup transportation in the event of an emergency. Test day is stressful enough without worrying over logistics!

4. Get a good night's sleep. Sleep is vitally important to the learning process. While the body sleeps, the brain actively processes information and resets for the next day. Always make sure that you consistently get a good night's sleep throughout your study period. Make sure to turn off electronics before bed, like computers, smart phones, televisions, and tablets. Electronics emit blue light that interferes with your body's ability to produce melatonin, a hormone responsible for regulating the body's internal clock.

Experts recommend that you should get at least eight hours of sleep every night. Here are some helpful tips if you typically have trouble sleeping:
- Avoid heavy snacks a couple of hours before going to bed.
- Do not consume any caffeine during the evening.
- Resist napping during the day.

If you still have trouble sleeping, try some deep breathing exercises, and try relaxing your muscles progressively in groups. The importance of sleep cannot be underestimated in the study process. You need to be as fresh as possible before battling with a difficult test. Also, remember to set an alarm to ensure that you wake up with enough time to get through your morning routine and depart on schedule.

5. Wear layered clothes to the test. No matter the season, layers are always the key to your test day wardrobe. There is no predicting the temperature at your test site. Even on the hottest days, the air conditioner could be on full blast, or a room heater could turn a frigid winter morning into a sauna. Wearing layers will protect you from being too cold or warm during the test. Wear comfortable shoes and avoid having on heavy jewelry or tight clothing. Always prioritize comfort over fashion when taking an exam.

6. Eat a healthy breakfast the morning of your exam. Test taking requires a lot of energy, so breakfast is an absolute must. You want your focus to be on the test, not on your hunger pangs. Consequently, selecting the right food is extremely important. Consider putting down the sugary cereals in place of a nutrient-dense meal that you're accustomed to. Also, be careful of consuming too much caffeine before the exam. Although you will initially feel alert, the inevitable crash will throw off your concentration later in the day.

Use the following checklist on the day before to make sure you are fully prepared for test day!

Checklist	
Enjoy a relaxing activity	
Reread the test instructions	
Prepare test materials and snack	
Verify the location of the test center and create a backup transportation plan in case of an emergency	
Lay out an outfit with multiple layers	
Set an alarm	
Turn off all electronics that emit blue light	
Go to bed at least eight hours before wakeup time	

7. Plan to arrive early to the test center. The test examiners will instruct you when to arrive for the test. Heed the advice of the examiners when they recommend how early to arrive. You should aim to arrive a half hour or so before the instructed time. You never know how long it will take to check-in. However, try not to arrive too early for the exam. You want to be early to avoid any unnecessary logistical anxiety, but not so early that you are needlessly sitting around and stressing out.

8. Stop drinking liquids an hour before the test and visit the bathroom before entering your designated test room. The clock is not your friend on test day. Although you might manage to complete every section with time to spare, you should try your best to conserve as much time as possible. Consequently, bathroom breaks should be avoided at all costs. Leaving your seat for any amount of time will reduce the time available to answer questions or double-check your answers. With that said, emergencies do happen, and you should obviously visit the bathroom if the need arises. However, if you stop drinking fluids an hour before the test and properly plan your bathroom breaks, then you will be in the best possible position to succeed.

Test-Taking Strategies

1. Remain as calm as possible. After spending hours on preparation, the pressure to perform can be overwhelming, but only if you let it. It is natural to be nervous, and those nerves are nature's way of keeping your mind sharp; however, it is important not to panic. Pay no attention to the other test takers; it does not matter how quickly other students finish. All that matters is that you keep calm,

Copyright © Mometrix Media. You have been licensed one copy of this document for personal use only. Any other reproduction or redistribution is strictly prohibited. All rights reserved.

mind the clock, and maintain a good pace. In addition, you should keep a positive outlook throughout the exam. If you do not believe that you will achieve your goals, then you will almost certainly be disappointed with your results. Be confident in your preparation and visualize a successful outcome. Here are some helpful tips if you struggle with anxiety during the exam:

- Take several deep breaths, exhale slowly, and imagine the stress leaving your body.
- Gently tap your feet on the floor if they become too restless. This will tire them out and allow you to focus. Similarly, if your hands become fidgety, tighten your fist as hard as possible, and then slowly release the pressure.
- Do not linger on difficult questions. One question will rarely make or break your final score. You do not want the stress from one question to transfer over to the next one. If you can go back on the test, mark the question and return to it later. Some separation will likely render the question more approachable.

Remember, at the end of day, it is just a test. No matter the results, everything will be fine; your life is not on the line.

2. Read the directions carefully. Although you have read the directions during your preparation, make sure to read the directions on test day. The directions will provide insight into how to approach the exam. Be sure to note how much time is allotted for each section and how the final score will be calculated. Aside from the written instructions, pay close attention to the verbal instructions provided by the proctor. In particular, determine whether the proctor will provide any verbal or written warning about the remaining time.

3. Read the whole question and each answer choice before making a selection. With multiple choice questions, you should be extremely careful of red herring answer choices. In order to reduce the possibility of falling into any traps, you should always read all of the answer choices before selecting your final answer, even if the answer seems obvious. Test writers fully realize that you are under time constraints, and therefore you will be more likely to rush through questions. Remember, tests are tricky by design, and you should be wary of answers that appear too obvious. Ruling out all of the answer choices will protect you from these tricks and raise your score!

4. Be an active reader and annotate the questions. Active reading will keep your mind fully alert during the test. You do not want to miss any clues provided by the test writers! You should be especially cautious of negative questions, like the "except" variety. Annotate the questions and answer choices by underlining, highlighting, and circling any key words. If provided, utilize the scrap paper or margins to jot down notes and outline long-form responses.

5. Utilize the process of elimination to narrow down the answer choices. The process of elimination is one of the most powerful tools at your disposal. Simply put, the process of elimination is a method of increasing your odds of selecting the correct answers by ruling out incorrect options. Many multiple-choice questions have at least one option that can be immediately eliminated. For example, an answer choice might be completely unrelated to the question. The process of elimination dramatically increases your odds of answering the question correctly. The more options that can be eliminated, the better your chances!

6. Look out for answer choices that are opposites. If two answer choices contradict each other, one of them must necessarily be incorrect. Although both choices could be incorrect, it is more probable that one will be correct.

7. Do not look for patterns in the answers. It is equally possible to have an equal distribution of answer choices or for one choice to appear three times as often as any other. The correct answers are randomly generated by a computer and should never be relied upon.

8. Review your work, if possible. Obviously, completing the test should be your first priority, but if you have any time remaining, use it to review your work. Resist the urge to leave the test site before time expires. Although leaving early might provide some early relief, you will regret not using all of your time if some silly mistake prevents you from achieving your goal. Catching a mistake can pay big dividends in your final score!

Run through these steps when reviewing your work:
1. Check to make sure that you answered every question. For long-form questions, check that you have addressed every sub-section of the question.
2. Check that you properly answered all of the negative questions, like "not true" and "except" questions. Failing to properly follow the question prompt will always result in an incorrect answer.
3. If you do not have time to review all answers, check the questions that gave you the most trouble.

FREE Study Skills DVD Offer

Getting the score you want on your exam can be tough, even with a good study guide. We offer a FREE Study Skills DVD to equip you with some solid study tips to help you prepare for your exam and achieve your goals on test day!

All that we ask is that you email us your feedback that would describe your experience so far with our product. To get your **FREE Study Skills DVD**, email freedvd@mometrix.com with "MY DVD" in the subject line and the following information in the body of the email:

- The name of the product you purchased.
- Your product rating on a scale of 1–5, with 5 being the highest rating.
- Your feedback. It can be long, short, or anything in-between, just your impressions and experience so far with our product. Good feedback might include how our study material met your needs and will highlight features of the product that you found helpful.
- Your full name and shipping address where you would like us to send your free DVD.

LSAT Information

The Law School Admission Test, or LSAT, is a requirement for application to all ABA-approved law schools. Test centers throughout the nation offer the LSAT in June, September or October, December, and February, and it is also available at many testing centers worldwide at the same time. And for those farther than one hundred miles from the nearest testing center, it may even be available for a fee at other locations.

Testing must be scheduled in advance, and is usually available only on specified Saturdays. However, students with religious prohibitions against Saturday events can apply to take the examination on the Monday following a regular Saturday test date. Accommodations can also be made for students with disabilities. Left-handed students can also request accommodation in seating, although such accommodations may depend on space. Candidates should be aware that the test day can take as long as five hours, with one 15-minute break after section three is administered.

The LSAT is a standardized collegiate examination, similar in construction to the Scholastic Aptitude Test (SAT). It provides a standard measure of the verbal and reasoning skills considered necessary for the legal profession. While most law schools require an applicant to have taken the LSAT no later than the December prior to anticipated admission, those who test earlier have a greater opportunity to redeem themselves in the event of a low score. In most cases, applicants are allowed to take the LSAT up to three times in any two-year period. Be aware, however, that not all schools go strictly by the highest score—some average all scores together. So, unless your score is many points below your goal, it may not be in your best interests to repeat the test. Check the procedure used at any schools you are applying to prior to repeating the test.

If you are reasonably certain you have bombed the test, you may also cancel your score entirely, provided your written request to do so is received immediately (prior to grading). This voids all record of your having taken the test. The test itself consists of five topical multiple-choice examinations. The exams contain Logical Reasoning, Reading Comprehension, and Analytical Reasoning questions. An experimental section of one of these types of questions is also included for field-testing future exam questions. The experimental section is not scored, but it is also not distinguishable from the scored sections. A sixth exam, an extemporaneous writing sample, is also on the exam, and is also not scored, but the text of the writing sample is sent along with the LSAT scores. Questions on the LSAT are created and administered by the Law School Admissions Council (LSAC), a nonprofit organization created in 1947 to standardize, facilitate, and improve the admission process for law schools nationwide.

Here are the different multiple-choice sections of the LSAT:
1. <u>Logical Reasoning/Arguments</u>: There are TWO sections of logical reasoning meant to test the applicant's ability to either draw reasonable conclusions from a valid argument or detect the fallacies in an invalid argument.
2. <u>Analytical Reasoning</u>: Sometimes called the Games section, this segment tests your ability to follow relationship structures throughout a written passage and properly account for the necessary parts using the conditions set.
3. <u>Reading Comprehension</u>: Precisely what it sounds like—this section tests how well you can read and understand various passages.

4. <u>Variable</u>: This is the ungraded section and can be Logical Reasoning, Analytical Reasoning, or Reading Comprehension. It is basically used to try out new test problems, but since you have no way of knowing which section is live and which is not, you should treat all sections as though they count toward your score.

Timing

It is generally recommended that students take the LSAT by the December before the fall semester the student intends to start. However, there are often benefits to taking the LSAT even earlier in the year; many advisors suggest taking the LSAT in June or October, thus giving students more time to prepare. To that end, students have a wide array of preparation options available, including practice exams, private and online tutoring, and courses designed to refresh and instruct students in the content areas and skills needed to succeed on the LSAT. Because of the nature of the material, and the amount of information that students assimilate, LSAC recommends that all students thoroughly prepare before taking the LSAT, even if they have high confidence in their mastery of the material.

Registering

The easiest and most often recommended method of registration is to create an LSAT student account and register online through the official LSAC Web site. The Web site allows students to select a test time, test center, and to pay for the exam fees with a credit card through the secure section of the site. Using online registration is recommended because many of the options that commonly need later modification—test time, test location, college codes, score report locations and so on—can easily be performed online with greater speed and efficiency than through the phone or mail.

For students who are unwilling or unable to sign up online, LSAC also allows for registration through the mail or by telephone. These methods are similar to the online account process, but are more inflexible and they less readily accommodate scheduling changes within the testing period. Students cannot withdraw or cancel registration during the regular registration period and register again for that same test during late period registration. For ease and efficiency of processing, online registration is advantageous and more accessible. Telephone system registration is available only from 8:30 AM to 4:45 PM (7:00 PM in the September-March time frame) and experiences peak traffic on Mondays (LSAC suggests contacting their offices later in the week to avoid the peak traffic experiences at the beginning of the week). Additionally, online registration is substantially faster because it doesn't require an application packet to be mailed and returned by the customer, as the phone registration and paper methods do.

Special circumstances

The LSAT testing process can accommodate students with disability, economic hardship, and geographic limitations. Here are a few of the options available for students who need accommodation in registering:

Fee waivers – Students who meet certain qualifications as listed on the official LSAC fee waiver form are eligible. The waivers cover the fees for two LSATs (taken within a two-year period), four college reports, and Law School Data Assembly Service (LSDAS) registration. LSAT waiver packets can be obtained through a variety of sources, including the admissions office of most law schools;

however, the basic criterion for a fee waiver is the absolute inability to pay. Thus, very few waivers are granted.

Non-Saturday testing – Students who have religious beliefs that prevent them from Saturday testing may apply for scheduled non-Saturday testing.

Geographic limitation - If a student cannot travel to a test center listed in the LSAC registration rolls (through disability or other disadvantage) and must travel more than 100 miles to a registered center listed with LSAC, students may apply to take the exam at a non-published test center. Students must contact LSAC at (215) 968-1001 to initiate the documentation process necessary to establish the need for a non-published test center. The student will be required to pay an additional fee for testing at a newly established location.

Disabled students – Students who have disabilities can apply for testing accommodation, including extended time periods and alternate testing formats. To establish eligibility for accommodation, the ACT Policy for Documentation requires that a disability be diagnosed and documented per specific requirements. Students should note that LSAC reserves the right to make final decisions about accommodation; therefore, we recommend that students prepare the necessary documentation and submit it well in advance.

Test Day

Materials needed

On test day, students need to have several items with them. There are three items that students can't do without: the test center admission ticket, without which the student can't take the test; a current form of government issued photo identification (a driver's license or current passport is sufficient), without which the student will not be admitted; and three or four soft-lead no. 2 pencils with erasers (no pens or mechanical pencils are allowed). Students must bring their own no.2 pencils to the test. The test proctor will not provide pencils. It is permissible to bring an analog watch. No digital timepieces, watches or timepiece displays are allowed.

The following materials may be taken into the testing room with the student, so long as they are stowed in a clear, plastic, sealable bag and placed under the student's seat during the test:
- LSAT Admission Ticket stub
- valid ID
- wallet
- keys
- analog wristwatch
- medical or hygiene products
- #2 or HB wooden pencils
- highlighter
- erasers
- pencil sharpener (no mechanical pencils)
- tissues
- beverage in plastic container or juice box (20 oz./591 ml maximum size) and snack for break only

During the exam, only the following items may be on the student's desktop, in addition to the test:

- tissues
- ID
- wooden pencils
- erasers
- pencil sharpener
- highlighter
- analog wristwatch

There are also specific things that students should **not** bring with them on test day. The following list, while not all-inclusive, covers the majority of items specifically forbidden for students to have with them during the LSAT exams:

- Books, including dictionaries
- Notes
- Scratch paper or other aids
- Colored pens or pencils
- Correction fluid
- Any electronic device (i.e. timer, phone, media player, PDA, camera)
- Reading material
- Tobacco in any form

Students should leave any items not specifically cited on the allowed materials list at home or in their vehicles during the testing period.

Identification

For the purposes of the LSAT, valid identification is assumed to mean a card, badge, or form that is a) issued by a governmental entity, b) current, meaning the identification was issued within the last two years, and c) bears a recognizable photo of the student, along with the student's first and last name (both names must be shown on the identification document) and the student's signature. Due to recent changes in LSAC policy regarding identification, only identification that meets all three criteria will be accepted as valid ID.

Common forms of acceptable identification include driver's licenses, passports, or another government-issued ID. There are several forms of identification that will not be accepted for the LSAT, and students need to be aware that they will not be admitted to the test center if they attempt to use an invalid form of identification. These invalid forms include out-of-date passports, LSAT admission tickets, learner's permits, birth certificates, Social Security cards, family portraits, Social Insurance cards, credit cards with photos, employee IDs, student IDs or any other form of identification that does not meet the three criteria outlined above.

Since the LSAT is only offered on certain dates, and since a student's delay in taking the test can adversely impact meeting deadlines for scholarship applications or admission requirements, it is vital that students include proper identification in the materials they bring to the test center. Packing an alternate form of identification in a bag with the materials the student brings to the test series is highly recommended.

Test day

The test day will begin with the student checking in before the assigned test time. For all exam periods except the June tests, students must report to the test center no later than 8:30 AM; for the June tests, students must report to the test center no later than 12:30 PM. The student will present their admission ticket and an acceptable form of identification to test center personnel, who will verify the validity of the information against a list of registered students. Once verified, the test center personnel will show the student to the test room and his or her assigned seat. The proctor will then provide the testing materials. At the assigned test time, the registered students will be allowed to start the exam.

After the third section is completed, the test proctor or center personnel will announce a short break—usually ten to fifteen minutes in length—during which all test materials will be collected. Test materials will remain in the custody of test center personnel during the break; students are permitted to walk around, stretch their legs, or use the restroom. No cell phones or other electronic devices may be used during the break, and students are not allowed to bring any food or drinks back to the test room. Per LSAT regulations, only those items brought to the test location in the previously described clear plastic bag are allowed. After the break, and after all test materials have been returned to the appropriate students, testing will resume. Most students should expect to take approximately five hours to complete the testing cycle, although this may vary from student to student.

Missed exam dates

There are several options available for students who miss taking the LSAT exam on the scheduled test date. The resolution of problems regarding missed exam dates depends upon the reasons for which the student is unable to attend, if severe weather or natural disaster prevents the student from reaching the center, it is likely the center itself will be closed, in which case the test will be rescheduled. If the test is held on the scheduled date, and the student is unable to arrive at the center at the appointed time, the student should immediately contact LSAC and review the available options. Students who miss their scheduled test date start times for other reasons—accidents, illness, tardiness, not having proper ID—have a different set of options to pursue. A student can request a late test date change, either through their LSAC student account, faxing LSAC at 215.968.1277 or by mailing a test change form to LSAC, Box 2000-T, Newtown, PA 18940. However, students should be aware that a $33 fee will be assessed if this option is pursued. When requesting a test date change, the applicant must provide all identifying information: student's name, address, LSAC account number, Social Security or Social Insurance number (or LSAC ID number), the test date, and the first and second choice regarding location. The request must be appropriately signed and dated. An additional option would be to request a refund, thereby canceling the appointment to take the LSAT altogether. Refunds can only be requested through written correspondence or through use of the LSAC Refund Request Form, both of which require the same information as the test date change. Only a partial refund of $45 will be given to students requesting refunds.

Misconduct

Law school applicants should be aware that the LSAC has established very stringent rules regarding possible misconduct during the LSAT. Since lawyers are expected to hold to a set of rigorous ethical standards, the application of those same high ethical standards applies to prospective law school applicants beginning with the application process. The official LSAC statement with regard to the

LSAT defines "misconduct" as: "the submission, as part of the law school admission process, including, but not limited to, regular, transfer, and visiting applications, of any information that is false, inconsistent, or misleading, or the omission of information that may result in a false or misleading conclusion, or the violation of any regulation governing the law school admission process, including any violation of LSAT test center regulations."

Because of the stringent standard, the types of behaviors which constitute misconduct under LSAC rules can be applied to a wider variety of offenses than would apply to other standardized tests. Specific actions that are considered misconduct by the LSAC include, but are not limited to, the following:

- submitting an altered or false transcript
- submitting an application with false, inconsistent, or misleading information
- submitting an altered, false, or unauthorized letter of recommendation
- falsifying records
- impersonating another applicant in taking the LSAT
- switching LSAT answer sheets with another applicant
- taking the LSAT for purposes other than applying to law school
- copying from others on the LSAT, or similar forms of cheating,
- obtaining advance access to test materials
- stealing test materials
- working, marking, erasing, reading, or turning pages on sections of the LSAT during unauthorized times
- submitting false, inconsistent, or misleading information to the LSDAS
- submitting false, inconsistent, or misleading statements or omissions of information requested on the LSAT & LSDAS Registration Form or on individual law school application forms
- falsifying transcript information, school attendance, honors, awards or employment
- providing false, inconsistent, or misleading information in the financial aid/scholarship application process

Charges of misconduct on the LSAT are very serious, and can be brought at any time: before a candidate's admission to law school, after admission and/or enrollment at a law school, even after passing the bar and admission to practice. If misconduct charges are brought against an applicant, the LSAC will immediately notify the school or schools in question. Pending reports and application package information will be halted until a member of the LSAC's Misconduct and Irregularities in the Admission Process Subcommittee has had a chance to investigate the allegations. The LSAC has procedural rules regulating the monitoring of misconduct investigations and guidelines for the methods to be employed. Those procedures begin once a representative has been assigned to investigate the allegation of misconduct.

Once the representative has concluded the investigation and reached a preliminary decision, the LSAC and the affected law schools are notified of the representative's findings, and the decision is appended to the applicant's LSAT and LSDAS reports. Depending on the determination of effect by the investigating representative, other agencies and governmental bodies may be informed as well. The LSAC has no authority to levy punishments or to advise and recommend disciplinary action. Disciplinary decisions are left entirely to the discretion of the affected schools. Since allegations of misconduct can occur at any phase of the law school application process, and extend even beyond the academic period, any violation of the stringent ethical standards of the legal profession can result in a range of penalties which may include:

- closing of a law school admission file
- revoking an offer of admission
- dismissal from law school via the school's internal channels
- disbarment

Preparation

Tips

Besides the studying and exam prep activities most students undertake before taking the LSAT, there are several basic steps students can take to help maximize their test results:

- Every test booklet has instructions on the front cover; read them carefully. Failure to follow instructions can result in incorrect results or dismissal for not abiding by them.
- Read every question carefully. In many cases the correct answer will depend on a nuanced interpretation of the material, so it is important to be clear on what is being asked.
- Be sure to take the test at a measured pace. There are dozens of questions to go through. Spending too much time on a single question or passage may negatively impact the amount of time left to resolve other questions.
- If the student finishes a test before time is called, it is advisable to go back through and review the answers. The student should use spare time to check the work and make corrections as necessary.
- Score sheets are read by computer, so it is vital that students make mark their answers neatly and with a minimum of smudging. If a mark requires erasure, the student must be sure that the mark is erased completely. Keep in mind that marks and notes made inside the test booklets are not counted toward your score, so make sure that all answers are recorded on the test sheet.
- Once time is called on an exam, students should put down their pencils and make no further marks on the sheet. Failure to do this will result in being dismissed from the exam and the score sheet being discarded.

<u>Writing prompt tips</u>

The writing prompt is forwarded to the LSAT test center as a digital image. Though the writing section is not scored, many law school admission offices do evaluate the writing prompt while reviewing the candidate's entire application packet. Therefore, LSAC strongly recommends students do their utmost to complete the writing prompt to the best of their ability in the allotted time. In addition to studying and exam prep activities, there are several basic steps students can take to help maximize their results on the LSAT writing prompt:

- Before starting to write the essay, take time to plan how you will present your supporting statements and the rationale for your conclusions as requested in the prompt. Take notes as needed, and follow these guidelines for your planning:
- Carefully consider the prompt. Make sure you understand the issue at stake. Read and think about it again if it seems unclear on the first read.
- Analyze your arguments and consider counter-arguments or flaws in the presentation of your response to questions. Try to address contradictions and weaknesses in your thinking so you can address them in writing the essay.
- Decide how your essay will be structured and organized.
- Outline the issue at the essay's beginning so readers will know you understand it.
- Use clear and logical steps to explain your position.
- Explain the issue's broader implications, or analyze it within a wider context, if possible.
- Present counter-arguments to the opposing views you noted before starting.
- Be specific whenever possible.
- Avoid monotony in your essay by using varied sentence length and structure. Along those lines, be careful to use precision in your word choices.
- Stay on-topic, and be sure your transitions from one thought to another and one paragraph to another are clear and reasonable.
- Be sure to present a strong and clear conclusion, reinforcing or summing up your argument in the process.
- If there is time, be sure to review the essay, correcting grammar and syntactical errors, illegible writing, punctuation, and errors in logic. Revisions should be done as neatly as possible.

A Further Look at the LSAT Sections

The LSAT is divided into five individual subject examinations, which cover a total of three skill areas. The material in each exam breaks down into the following categories:

Logical Reasoning – Students are tested on the ability to evaluate, critically analyze, and complete a number of arguments. The questions require the test-taker to read and understand a short passage, and then respond to questions on the passage in a manner which demonstrates logical and critical thought processes. The examination passages require the student to identify the basic assumptions of the argument and other possible conclusions which may be drawn from it. In addition, the student will be asked to identify specific issues presented in the argument, and to formulate parallel arguments which can be made, or to reveal supporting statements which either strengthen or weaken the argument. These skill areas are covered in two separate examinations.

Analytical Reasoning – Students are tested on the ability to examine a table or set of relationships between entities and draw logical conclusions about the relationships. The test, often termed the Games section, is designed to measure the ability to logically analyze complex legal situations. The question format of this section presents a set of initial conditions, followed by a set of rules governing those conditions, and then a prompt for the student to develop reasonable and logical conclusions based on the circumstances, conditions, and rules provided. Follow-up questions may revise or modify the initial set of circumstances, rules, or conditions, requiring students to reorganize and develop new conclusions.

Reading Comprehension – Students are tested on direct reading comprehension and the identification of inferences based on the material presented. The test consists of several prose passages from various academic disciplines, which then are followed by several questions on the passage or selected parts of the passage. The exam calls for the student to draw conclusions based on understanding of the primary argument, and to locate specific information within the passages, or to demonstrate comprehension of the overall structure of the selection. Since reading skills such as determining the main idea and understanding causal relationships are being tested, rote fact checking is not included in the exam.

Unscored section – This section is used to test potential future questions or new test formats. The results of the unscored section are not included in the student's final test score. The section is not identified during the exam, but is generally among the first three sections administered to avoid question fatigue. The unscored section can contain questions covering any of the skill areas addressed in the regular LSAT course.

Writing prompt

The writing prompt is a short written exercise that is given at the end of the regular exam. The prompt is not scored; instead, a digital copy is made and sent along with the test scores to the law schools to which the student is applying. The writing exam consists of a decision prompt, which provides a problem for the student to examine and a set of criteria that can be used to analyze the issue and come to a conclusion. The students must write an essay using the criteria and defend their decisions in writing. The problem the student must analyze is generally a non-controversial issue which encourages dispassionate critical analysis and logical written argument. For a short time, LSAC included an alternate type of prompt called an argument prompt—wherein a student had to analyze a logical argument similar to those seen in the logical reasoning exams and critique the argument—but that prompt was retired as of June 2007. The decision prompt used currently for the writing exam reflects a formal standard adopted at the LSAT's inception.

Students should be aware that, while the writing prompt is included with the LSAT score, not all law schools place value upon the writing exercise because it does not carry a score. In any case, most law schools require a personal statement as part of the admission packet. However, many law schools do place value on the writing prompt and the writing exam is evaluated as a vital part of the LSAT for the majority of prospective law students.

Number of questions

Individual test times will depend on several factors—the student's reading speed, level of comfort with the material, preparation time—but the allotted time is the same. Including break time between tests, students can count on the allotted time being approximately five hours. The LSAC recommends students pace themselves accordingly. Students who begin testing on the standard LSAT exam series at 8:30 AM can expect to be finished with the exam no later than 3:30 PM.

Each section of the exam is allotted 35 minutes, including the writing prompt. The number of questions can vary, but in general, each multiple-choice section of the LSAT will have between 15 and 25 questions, depending on the complexity of the passage and the difficulty of questions asked. Thus, the average LSAT test-taker can expect to answer a minimum of 75 and a maximum of 125 questions over the period of the test day. Keep in mind that not only does the number of questions vary, but so does the number of questions in each section. While there are two sections of logical reasoning, the experimental section (which is not scored, but is also not identified as such to the student) may draw from any subject in the regular exam series. Consequently, two test-takers on the same day may experience great variation in the number and emphasis of questions being posed during the LSAT series. Since scoring is the same regardless of what questions were asked, students are strongly urged to become familiar with the concepts and practices of each of the subject areas before taking the exams.

Results

Students who create an electronic account with LSAT can generally view their scores online within three to four weeks of the test. While most scores will be made available online at this time, there is no guarantee that scores will be posted within this estimated timeframe. Unless there is an issue that delays the reporting—inconsistent information on the registration forms and test booklet, delay in delivering the test sheets to the scoring center, issues raised by test center personnel and the like—scores will be made available no later than eight weeks from testing. Students should also note that online posting of test scores does not provide a speed advantage in reporting scores to law schools.

In addition to online reporting and mailed reports, students can elect to use TelScore, a telephone reporting service, to obtain their reports if they do not have Internet access. To use TelScore, students must call 215.968.1200; if students need assistance, calling 215.968.1001 between 8:30 AM to 4:45 PM (ET) April–August and 8:30 AM to 7:00 PM (ET) September–March will get the student in touch with a representative.

The scoring process cannot be expedited in any way. Regardless of circumstances, the scores for the LSAT exams cannot be tallied and made available to students sooner than three weeks after the test. Only students with valid student LSAT online accounts can check their scores online; all other students must call TelScore to get their scores or wait for their score reports to arrive in the mail.

If necessary, students can cancel their LSAT scores if they feel their scores are not worthy of reporting. This can be done at the time of the exam itself; instructions for score cancellation are provided on the back of the answer sheet. If the student chooses to cancel score reporting of a test, it is vital that all instructions are precisely followed; otherwise, the score will be reported. Since score cancellations marked on the answer sheets are processed with the regular LSAT test sheets, confirmation of score cancellations will not be issued until approximately four to five weeks after the test date.

If the student decides later (within a week of taking the LSAT) to cancel scoring, the student can petition LSAC to cancel scores via signed fax, overnight letter, or the Score Cancellation Form available directly from LSAC. Requests submitted by these alternative methods must be received by LSAC within six calendar days of taking the test, or the test will be scored per usual procedure. Any request for score cancellation, regardless of the method used, must include the student's signature for it to be considered a valid cancellation request by LSAC.

Copyright © Mometrix Media. You have been licensed one copy of this document for personal use only. Any other reproduction or redistribution is strictly prohibited. All rights reserved.

Score ranges

Like most admission exam, the LSAT is a standardized test. This means that raw scores are generally adjusted by a formal statistical process to achieve a normal range. In the case of the LSAT, the scores are equated, or adjusted to minimize differences which result from differing question banks and/or administrations of the exam. The range of adjusted scores falls into a 60-point range. A score of 120 is the lowest possible score; 180 is the highest possible score.

The raw score is computed by tallying the number of correctly answered questions. There is no penalty for guessing, and there is no difference in weighting between individual questions from different sections of the LSAT. On average, the percentile scores generally break down as follows:

Score	Percentile (rank relative to other students)
151	50th percentile
164	90th percentile
173	99th percentile
178	99.9th percentile

The first year of law school is considered to be the most grueling. While strong performance on LSAT and other performance factors like undergraduate GPA remain controversial barometers of student success, LSAC maintains that LSAT performance has a fairly strong correlation to success in law school. Consequently, LSAT scores are one of the most critical admissions factors for law school entry, along with undergraduate GPA. The performance scores on LSAT, combined with undergraduate GPA scores, are also considered a reliable indicator of bar passage, as well as a predictor of overall law school GPA.

Score computation

Scoring for the LSAT is done in a phased process. The first step is to evaluate the student's answer sheet and tally the correct answers. There is no penalty for incorrect answers; those questions are simply ignored for the purposes of scoring. Once the raw scores have been tallied, the raw scores are then converted into a normalized measure of how well those scores reflect performance yardsticks developed through past score analysis. This process is called equating, and yields a statistical breakdown of the scores. The results are considered valid across test dates and test versions, meaning that any given score is equivalent to the same numerical score achieved on a different testing date and a different exam version.

Once the test scores are equated, a model resembling a bell curve is constructed and the final scores are derived. The result is expressed as a score falling between 120 and 180. Because the scores are expressed in statistical models and not pure raw scores, there can be varying degrees of missed responses between different scores. For example, scores of five points' difference in the 95th percentile might differ by three questions, meaning the student who received a 178 may have answered three more questions correctly than a student with a 173 score. On the other hand, scores closer to the median (closer to the center of the bell curve) may differ by more; a student with a 155, for example, may have answered nine more questions correctly than a student scoring 150.

Disputing a score

If a student feels that a question was scored incorrectly, the student can request that LSAC review the question or questions presented. To generate the review, the student must file a written inquiry with LSAC within 90 days of receiving a score report. This inquiry must specifically state the objection or challenge. The student must be clear in "stating and supporting the reasons why the credited response is not the one and only best answer to the question," as required by LSAC policy. The request for review will then be subject to a three-tiered review process. If the review request is found to have merit regarding the issue raised, corrective action will be initiated.

Moreover, if an event or disruption at the test center—including cancellations, mistimings, deviations from standard procedure, indications of advance knowledge of exam content, or other compromises of the process —LSAC will investigate the matter. If any procedural violations are determined to be the fault of LSAC or the test center, LSAC will consider solutions and offer students an array of possible remedial actions, at the discretion of LSAC.

The student must be aware that LSAC maintains a rigorous ethical standard for both prospective law school applicants and admitted students. Deviations or lapses in these ethical standards are punishable by a variety of disciplinary options, including revocation of admission, closing of an application file, and in some cases, disbarment. Students are strongly advised to familiarize themselves with LSAC ethical standards and guidelines before registering or even beginning to prepare for the LSAT.

Organizations

LSDAS

The Law School Data Assembly Service (LSDAS) is a centralized organization established for providing a standardized format for the evaluation and submission of undergraduate records of law school applicants. It is intended to simplify the overall application process and to ensure fairness by providing a baseline metric for evaluating undergraduate transcripts. Virtually all ABA-approved law schools require applicants to sign up with the Law School Data Assembly Service. Unlike American law schools, Canadian law schools do not participate in or otherwise provide information to the LSDAS, and do not require applicants to use it or register with the service.

The primary function of the Law School Data Assembly Service in the law school application process is in the preparation of the performance report sent to each law school to which an applicant submits scores and other data. Each report contains the student's application, personal essay, and as many letters of recommendation that the student provides. In addition to the student-created material, the report also contains an undergraduate academic summary. This summary is made up of all undergraduate, graduate, or other pertinent transcripts. The academic records of other professional or law schools previously attended are also compiled and sent, along with LSAT scores and copies of the writing sample that accompanies the LSAT. Additional supporting information, such as letters of recommendation, is also included in the report. Although Canadian law schools do not participate in the Law School Data Assembly Service, they do receive an LSAT score report and copies of the writing sample.

As with the LSAT, there is no specific timetable for LSDAS registration. That decision is entirely up to the student, and will be contingent upon a variety of factors. LSDAS registration should coincide with the student's chosen exam schedule, the availability of letters of recommendation, and other submission package requirements. However, LSAC advises that law school applicants register a minimum of four to six weeks prior to the application deadlines of the law schools where they intend to apply. In general, it takes roughly two weeks to prepare transcripts from the point where they are received to the point where they are finally processed into an LSDAS report.

It is important for applicants to remember that, although LSDAS is a necessary step for applying to ABA-approved law schools, the LSDAS registration process is separate from the law school application. The fees also are separate. Paying the fee for LSDAS registration does nothing to meet the fee requirements of the law school application. The separate fee structures required for LSDAS registration and for law school application is an area often misunderstood by law school applicants. When sending in the fee for LSDAS registration, students are strongly advised to adhere to their prospective law school's policies and deadlines regarding the separate application processes and fees. Also, if applying to more than one law school, it is important that students make sure that enough LSDAS reports are ordered. One LSDAS report must accompany each individual law school application.

If a student needs to order additional LSDAS reports, there are three ways to do so. The quickest and most efficient way is to order them through the student's online account, if applicable. If the student does not have an online account, a second method of ordering would be to use the form included in the current LSAT/LSDAS registration packet. That form must be completely and accurately filled out, and submitted via mail or fax. If the form is not available for any reason, then applicants can call LSAC at 215.968.1001 and speak to a representative, who will assist the applicant with the ordering process. Since the lines are not staffed on a 24/7 basis, this is the least flexible and least preferred option.

Applicants do not have to inform LSAC of which schools to send LSDAS reports directly. When an applicant submits the application material to a law school or a group of law schools, those schools contact LSAC and request the relevant reports directly. Again, it is imperative that the student have ordered enough reports to accommodate the number of law schools applied to. If a student has not ordered and paid for the correct number of reports, the transmission of those reports to the appropriate law school admission offices will be delayed. Occasionally, additional information will need to be appended to reports. When this occurs, an updated report will be sent to the law schools identified by the applicant. These updates will be performed at no additional charge to the applicant.

LSAC

The Law School Admissions Council (LSAC) is a nonprofit organization created in 1947 to standardize, facilitate, and improve the admission process for law schools nationwide. In addition, the LSAC provides a number of services and programs related to legal education, such as the creation and administration of the LSAT, operation of the LSDAS, law school forums for educators and students, and operation and maintenance of the Candidate Referral Service (CRS).

The CRS is valuable because it allows applicants to release pertinent biographic, academic, and employment information to schools which are trying to match students with their own recruitment needs. CRS also disseminates information about the student's law school preferences so that schools meeting these preferences may contact the applicant directly. LSAC comprises all law schools approved by the ABA, as well as a number of Canadian law schools recognized by a provincial or territorial law society or government agency (fifteen at the present time), all of which are included in the voting membership of the Council.

While the LSAC is intimately involved in all aspects of the application standardization process, from developing LSAT exams and test prep materials to providing database services to law schools and their admission offices, it is important to note that the LSAC is in no way involved in individual assessments of an applicant's readiness for law school. LSAC provides a fair, level ground for applicants and law schools to evaluate information, but each law school makes its own decisions regarding applicant suitability. Aside from providing general information, LSAC has no input into the law school selection process.

Reading Comprehension Test

The Reading Comprehension section of the LSAT is designed to test your abilities to understand and interpret written materials. Lawyers daily perform interpretation of written information, much of which can be difficult to understand. Reading comprehension skills are critical for success in law school, as students are required to read and understand massive amounts of material. Even though almost all law school applicants are aware that they'll have to do a lot of reading if they're admitted, many law school graduates still report being shocked at finding out just how much reading they were going to be required to do. The Reading Comprehension section of the LSAT is designed to weed out those applicants who don't have the skills to cope with the reading requirements of law school.

On this portion of the LSAT, you will have 35 minutes to answer approximately 27 questions about four reading assignments. Three of these assignments will consist of only one passage, while one will be a comparative reading test, consisting of two passages. The passages are usually between 400 to 500 words in length, and subject matter can be in any field, but most passages are about a topic in law, science, or the liberal arts. You will not need to know any specialized information to understand a passage, even if it includes technical terms you have never encountered before. You are expected to base your answers only on what is stated or implied in the passage or passages.

One aspect of the Reading Comprehension test that makes it so difficult is that you're expected to read and comprehend a large amount of difficult material in a very brief amount of time. Each passage you'll tackle will be hundreds of words long, and will often be quite ponderous. Passages are almost always densely written, filled with facts and details which may or may not be important for you to remember. The sheer amount of information in a passage can be quite intimidating and unnerving to test takers.

Then, once you've finally navigated your way through the passage, you're confronted with up to eight questions you must answer. Each question will have four possible answers to choose from, and many of them will be obtuse, having been deliberately crafted to be very hard to interpret. Sometimes it will seem as if several answer choices could conceivably be acceptable. For many questions, two answer choices will be so similar that choosing one or the other would seem to be little different than flipping a coin. You will have less than nine minutes to read each passage thoroughly, mark important information, read each question and all four answer choices, compare and contrast the possible answers with each other, and go back to the passage to find the answer. This is a formidable challenge, to put it mildly. There's no denying that the LSAT Reading Comprehension section is a race against the clock; in fact, it's designed to be that way.

However, there's no reason you need to fear the Reading Comprehension test. Yes, it's hard, but in this guide, we'll show you how you can excel on this portion of the LSAT. You'll learn:

- the main question types
- the best plan for tackling the reading material
- powerful reading techniques
- what to focus on in your reading
- what notes to take
- "red flag words" to watch for
- how these "red flag words" can point you to the correct answer

- other factors that can be important signals
- how to choose between answers that are extremely similar
- and much more...

The Passages: What's the Deal?

The passages you'll encounter on the LSAT Reading Comprehension test are unlikely to be similar to any of your regular reading material. In fact, it's very likely you have never run across any of these kinds of passages before. They are usually taken from academic journals, and then adapted for use on the LSAT. They have to be carefully edited and rewritten to suit the 400-500 word format used for Reading Comprehension passages. Any parts requiring technical knowledge on the part of the reader are removed.

That's just the beginning. After any information only understandable by a professional in the field has been excised, the material then must be rewritten to work around the sentences or paragraphs that got removed. Sometimes the results are less than ideal, which explains why LSAT Reading Comprehension passages sometimes seem jarring and disjointed. The reason the passages are so dense is that the editors at the Law School Admissions Council have taken most of the details and facts from an article that was 1500-2000 words and forced them into a passage that is only about a third or fourth as long.

Topics can be all over the map, but most of the time the subject of the reading passage will not be something you are familiar with, but an obscure topic. This is done deliberately to keep the Reading Comprehension test fair. By choosing subject matter that virtually all test takers are unfamiliar with, the test creators make the exam a level playing field where no one has an advantage because they know the subject better than others.

When you add all these factors up – scholarly writing, three or four pages worth of material crammed into a one page article, and subject matter that isn't even on the average person's radar – it becomes clear that the passages you'll be dealing with on this part of the LSAT are not exactly light reading. Knowing these things before you take the LSAT will help keep you from feeling overwhelmed when you begin this section. You can relax knowing that you're not supposed to be familiar with the material, that it's supposed to be awfully dense, and that everyone else is in the same boat you are.

There's more good news – the LSAT doesn't penalize incorrect answers. In other words, if you choose the wrong answer, it doesn't lower your score. If you're running out of time, and a question completely stumps you, just pick a letter and fill it in. You may get lucky and get it right; if not, there's no harm done, because a wrong answer is scored the same as a blank answer. It won't raise your score, of course, but it won't lower it either, as your score is based only on correct answers. Another thing to keep in mind is the fact that the LSAT is not scored the same way a typical test is scored. It's a scaled score, and that's very good news if you're the kind of person who tends to worry every time you're not completely sure that an answer is correct. Because of the scaled scoring, a person can get over 40% of the answers wrong and still receive a score that's about average. Of course, an average LSAT score is not going to help your application stand out, but that's missing the point. The important thing is that you shouldn't worry too much about getting an occasional answer wrong. Because if you can miss nearly half the questions and still receive a score that's near the average, just think how high your score can be if you diligently prepare for the exam.

The Big Picture: How to Approach the Reading Comprehension Questions

There are several factors that will contribute to your success on the Reading Comprehension portion of the LSAT, and the first one is having a definite plan for tackling each question from the beginning. Knowing exactly what you're going to do prevents you from wasting time by trying to decide on a plan of attack at the last minute, or even worse, trying out different approaches to each question. These are critical mistakes that many test takers make, resulting in a lower score on the LSAT than they could have achieved had they been better prepared.

One Very Important Tip

There are several different approaches you could take to the material, but they aren't all equally effective. In fact, there's one popular approach that is almost guaranteed to waste time and cause confusion if you follow it. We'll look at the various approaches and compare and contrast their strengths and weaknesses in a moment. Before we do, here's one easy rule to help you save time on the Reading Comprehension section:

Do not waste time reading the instructions.

That's right – you should not read the instructions at the beginning of the Reading Comprehension section. You should familiarize yourself with them right now. The instructions have been the same for decades, and there's no reason to think they're going to change any time soon. They aren't complicated at all, so just learn them now and you won't lose any time on test day by taking time to read them two or three times to make sure you're not missing anything. Here are the official instructions which appear at the beginning of the Reading Comprehension section on every LSAT.

Each set of questions in this section is based on a single passage or a pair of passages. The questions are to be answered based on what is <u>stated</u> or <u>implied</u> in the passage or pair of passages. For some of the questions, more than one of the choices could conceivably answer the question. However, you are to choose the best answer; that is, the response that most accurately and completely answers the question, and blacken the corresponding space on your answer sheet.

That's pretty simple and easy to remember. So, learn the directions now and save valuable time on the LSAT.

What Are Your Options?

There are several approaches you can take when you turn to a passage on the Reading Comprehension section. You can start by:
  A. jumping right in - reading the passage and then answering the questions
  B. skimming the passage, then skimming the questions, answering the easy ones, then reading the passage in full and answering the rest of the questions
  C. reading the first and last sentence of each paragraph of the passage, then reading the passage in full and going on to answer the questions
  D. reading the questions so that you can look for the answers on your first reading of the passage, then reading the passage and answering the questions

These approaches have their proponents, but there are a lot of reasons to believe that A is the best option. Most people will be more successful if they take a straightforward approach by simply reading the passage and then answering the questions. Now, there's more to "reading" a passage than simply reading it, and we'll get to that. But first, let's look at the different approaches to see how they compare with each other.

We've already told you that A is the best, so let's start with B. Skimming is often recommended for picking up the gist of material quickly, and in many cases, it works very well. So why don't we recommend it for the LSAT Reading Comprehension exam? There are two reasons: First, because the passages you'll be dealing with on the LSAT, unlike most of the reading material you've encountered before, don't lend themselves to skimming. The second problem amplifies and exacerbates the first one – the correct answers to the questions usually don't involve the kind of information you can pick up by skimming.

Pick up any newspaper and start skimming the main article on the front page, and it's easy to get the gist of it – the President signed a bill requiring better nutritional labeling at fast food restaurants, for example. You may miss the fact that he signed it at an elementary school and not in a Rose Garden ceremony, and you may not notice that the bill only passed by a very slim margin in the Senate, or that three Republican senators broke ranks and voted with the Democrats. But you'll pick up and retain the main information. The same goes for most magazine articles, blog posts, and even many books. In these cases, skimming can be quite effective when you want the big picture and you want it fast.

LSAT Reading Comprehension passages aren't anything like newspaper articles or blog posts, unfortunately. They are so stuffed with information and detail that skimming them is worse than an exercise in futility. Skimming is for articles that use every day English and contain a few important facts, which are easily picked out and remembered. The passages on the LSAT are dense and difficult to follow, they make complex arguments on different levels, and they almost always rely on technical jargon and/or a highly advanced vocabulary to do so. You won't learn a thing by skimming them, because you *can't*. On the contrary, you'll probably find yourself getting lost and going over the same material several times, which defeats the whole purpose. Second, skimming on tests is best suited for answers to very basic questions. Many exams have questions which simply ask a person to locate information in the text, and don't require any analysis. Questions such as "How old was Beethoven when he wrote his first composition?", "Which continent has the greatest land mass?", and "Who was the last person to arrive at the scene?" are easy to answer by skimming. You won't be seeing any questions of that type on the LSAT Reading Comprehension test.

What's wrong with C? There are a couple of drawbacks to this approach. The Reading Comprehension passages are dense precisely because the individual sentences are dense. If you try to decipher one of these sentences you're going to run into the same problem as the person trying to skim – to get anything out of a stand-alone sentence at all, you will most likely have to read it more than one time. Even reading it several times, however, is unlikely to be any more effective. That's because each sentence after the first one interacts with and builds on the foundation laid by all the previous sentences. One sentence simply won't make much sense by itself. Trying to glean some insights into the meaning of the passage by reading the first and last sentences of each paragraph won't yield any meaningful information, because without the details and context from the rest of the paragraph these sentences will be essentially unintelligible.

Just as with skimming, the idea behind the first sentence/last sentence approach is basically sound when it comes to other kinds of reading material. In most kinds of non-fiction writing, the author often puts the main idea of the paragraph in the opening sentence, and often reiterates or stresses it in the closing sentence. However, not only are the LSAT Reading Comprehension passages too dense and complex for this to work, the LSAT writers are aware of the popularity of this strategy and they take pains to foil it. So, even in the rare cases when a sentence might concisely express the main idea, it's unlikely to be the first or last one of the passage.

Option *D* also looks promising at first glance; in fact, reading the questions before reading the passage might well be the optimum strategy on most reading comprehension tests. When the reading material is not very complex, it makes perfect sense to find out what you need to look for prior to reading the passage. This greatly simplifies your task, and can be a real time saver.

On the LSAT Reading Comprehension, however, reading the questions first and then the passage is a recipe for disaster. On average, each passage will have seven questions, none of which will be easy. Each one will require careful, focused thought just to make sure you've understood the question precisely. In some cases, merely reading the question won't be enough - you'll need to read, consider, and compare and contrast the answer choices with each other to even have an idea what you should be looking for when you read the passage.

For example, many questions will be some variation of "What is the author's main point?" followed by five answer choices. The five choices will each be lengthy, and a few of them will be remarkably similar. Since you should be able to understand the author's main point by reading the passage, what would you gain by trying to do so while simultaneously attempting to mentally keep several different and highly nuanced answer choices separate as you read? If that doesn't sound difficult enough, imagine trying to do the same thing for up to eight different questions as you read the passage for the first time. For most people, even remembering all the questions while reading the passage would be extremely difficult. Doing so while also keeping a couple dozen answer choices in mind at the same time is simply impossible. It's difficult to see how reading the questions before the passage can increase a person's comprehension of a difficult reading selection. On the contrary, using this strategy on the LSAT would almost certainly have a significant negative impact on a person's comprehension and retention of what they've read.

The best option, by far, is *A* – start by reading the passage in its entirely, and only then start answering the questions. Once you've finished the passage, you should start with the first question and answer it before moving on to the next one, and then answer each question in turn. Don't bother skimming the questions to see if there are some easy ones you can answer first before concentrating on the harder ones. That won't work, for the same reason skimming the passage itself won't work. There are very few easy questions on the LSAT Reading Comprehension exam. Most questions are either difficult, or extremely difficult. If you encounter a question that's particularly difficult, move on to the next one. Never forget that you're in a race against the clock. If you're running out of time and still have some unanswered questions left, just take a guess and fill in a circle. Of course, when you stick with this approach, you'll have a much better chance of answering all the questions compared to using any of the other ones, because they simply eat up too much time.

So, when it comes to the LSAT Reading Comprehension a simple, straightforward approach is best. You should read the passage first. Only after that should you even look at the questions. Any other approach will waste valuable time and make answering the questions much more difficult. We think it's pretty clear why the simple approach of reading the passage in its entirety before even looking at the questions is the best one. However, in case you still have any doubts, the Law School Admission Council, the organization that creates the LSAT, also recommends this approach as being the most effective.

There's a Lot More to Reading Than Just Reading

What is the most important skill for achieving a high score on the Reading Comprehension section? That's easy – it's being very good at "active reading." If reading isn't one of your strong suits, now's the time to start working on that. Anyone with average to poor reading skills simply won't have a chance to succeed on this portion of the LSAT without significant improvement between now and test day. However, this doesn't mean that if you possess superior reading skills that you can relax or that the Reading Comprehension exam will be a breeze for you. You may have a leg up on someone with mediocre reading skills, but odds are you're not used to doing the kind of reading that's necessary for success on the LSAT Reading Comprehension test.

The kind of reading needed for success on the LSAT, active reading, is much different than the kind of reading most people are used to, and that includes even those very good readers who have high natural or acquired abilities for comprehension and retention. It's far from being the same kind of activity a person engages in when they curl up with a good book. You may have already used a form of active reading when you underlined important passages in textbooks, but active reading involves a lot more than that. Active reading is work, and to get good at it takes practice.

So, what is active reading all about? Let's start by talking about its opposite. How many times have you been reading a magazine, book or newspapers and had to stop and start over from the beginning because you realized that you had no idea what you'd just read over the last few minutes? This has happened to virtually everyone, and it happens on a regular basis. In fact, it's not uncommon for people to have to start over several times before the material finally starts registering with their brain. That's because our mind has a natural tendency to wander while we're reading. If what we're reading is emotionally gripping, such as a key passage in a mystery novel, or extremely interesting in other ways, our mind tends to overcome this tendency and we have no trouble staying focused on the material.

Of course, most of the time people fall somewhere between these two extremes when it comes to staying focused while reading. We usually comprehend and retain some of what we read without having to force ourselves. That won't be good enough for the LSAT. The passages you'll be reading in the Reading Comprehension portion of the exam will be neither interesting nor emotionally gripping. They will be exceedingly dry and dull, in addition to being extremely dense, which will make for very tedious reading. It will take a strenuous effort to stay focused on the exam.

That's the beauty of active reading – it forces you to mentally dive into the passage and actively involve yourself in the text. There are both mental and physical aspects of active reading. Both aspects are important, but it's the physical part that plays a bigger role in enabling you to come back and find the information you're looking for after reading the questions. However, in this case, the whole is truly greater than the sum of its parts. It's the combination of keeping both your mind and your hand fully engaged in the text that makes active reading so powerful.

Active Reading: The Mental Aspect

As you read each passage, you'll want to keep several questions in mind:
- What is the author's main point?
- What is the author's point of view?
- What is the author's tone?
- What are some of the author's key arguments?
- What are some other viewpoints the author takes note of?

Keeping these questions in mind isn't difficult, although it might seem that way at first glance. If you think about it, however, most of them are questions that will naturally come to mind any time a person is reading a text he's unfamiliar with. When we read something for the first time we tend to automatically ask ourselves what the author is trying to say and where he's coming from, and we take notice of his tone and the points he's making. Unfortunately, we also tend to brush these things away while we're reading, and that's one of the main reasons we find it so easy to get completely distracted.

You can avoid this problem by choosing to deliberately focus on these questions as you read. If you have this as a clear and definite purpose in your mind as you begin, staying focused and on track for the few minutes it takes to read each passage will not be a problem. This is another reason you should not read the LSAT Reading Comprehension questions before reading the passage. You'll have plenty of questions to be thinking about as you read without adding five to eight more, along with a couple dozen possible answer choices to consider. It will be a challenge to keep the above questions in mind as you read and interpret the passage, but you can do it if you make a serious effort.

There is one more important consideration when it comes to active reading on the exam, and that's how to handle words you're unfamiliar with. These will fall into two categories. The first one is technical jargon relevant to the context of the passage, but unknown to the average person. The second category will consist of advanced vocabulary words of a non-technical nature. Hopefully, most of the unfamiliar words you encounter on the LSAT will fall into the first category. Don't let these worry you, as they will either be explained in the passage, either implicitly or explicitly, or they will be of no importance. As for the non-technical words you run into, if they're not explained explicitly you can often infer their meaning from the context. If you do happen to run into a word and you have absolutely no idea what it means, and the context is no help whatsoever, don't stress about it, as it's unlikely that any questions are going to be based on it.

Active Reading: The Physical Aspect

As you have probably surmised, the physical aspect of active reading involves annotation, or marking up the text. You won't be provided any blank paper during the Reading Comprehension exam for notes, but you will be allowed to makes notes in the text itself, and you'll want to make effective use of the power of annotation. Making the right kinds of notes and markups in the text will enable you to track down the answers to questions much, much faster.

Now, if you've bought a few used textbooks in your academic career, you're no doubt aware that annotation can be taken way too far. Those unfortunate souls who underline nearly every sentence on a page, or even sometimes in a whole chapter, have done themselves no good at all, and only wasted their time. The whole point of marking up a text is to make a word or passage stand out from the whole. If everything on a page has been highlighted, then nothing has been highlighted. That shouldn't be a problem for you with the Reading Comprehension passages, but you should keep in mind that it's easy to make too many notations. Just make sure you don't go overboard and slow yourself down. Also, be as legible as possible. Many of your notations will be a letter or two, or a symbol or numeral, so make sure you can read them with one quick glance. You don't want to be struggling to decipher your own handwriting when seconds count.

What kind of things should you be noting, and how should you mark them? There are several things you'll want to keep an eye out for as you read. You'll want to be on the lookout for certain kinds of words or phrases which can be important guideposts when it comes to answering the questions. They show that something is coming that will emphasize an author's point more strongly, or support his argument, or mark a shift of some sort in the writing, such as contrasting or comparing one thing with another. Think of them as "red flags", because they are often important signals that you ignore or skip over at your own peril.

Here are some of the main ones to watch for:

Words that signal emphasis: additionally, also, furthermore, in addition

Words that signal support: because, for example, since, regardless

Words that signal a shift in thought: but, after all, in spite of, except, yet, although, admittedly, on the other hand, despite, whereas, still, however, nonetheless, in contrast, even though, nevertheless, unlike

---

Marking these red flags so they stand out will make it easier to find the correct answer for many of the questions when the answer isn't immediately clear to you. You can circle or underline these words. Using circles might make the words stand out more, but underlining them takes less time.

You also need to highlight the author's main point as soon as you come across it. You could draw a circle around the sentence or sentences that make up the main point, but that would be time consuming. It's best to use some sort of abbreviation such as "MP" off to the side of the key passage.

Sometimes the author will include a number of supporting arguments, points, reasons, etc. You can number these off to the side.

When a passage on the Reading Comprehension exam offers a definition, there's a good chance that the definition will be important. Mark it with a "D" off to the side.

Most passages will feature points or arguments that oppose or conflict with the main point the author is making. Mark these with an "O" off to the side.

Some parts of the passage will likely compare and contrast an argument and a counter-argument, and these sections are usually important. Mark them with a "C" off to the side.

Obviously, in some parts of some passages, you'll encounter more than one thing that needs to be spotlighted, meaning you'll have several notations off to the side in the same part of the passage. This could be quite confusing, which would defeat the purpose of these annotations, so it's best to use an arrow connecting the letter, letters, or number to the appropriate part of the passage. If necessary, use parentheses or brackets to enclose the important sentence or sentences to make it clear exactly what an arrow is pointing to. These enclosures should be used only when necessary, however, because of the time factor.

You will be issued a highlighter and a #2 pencil to use during the exam. You can use both of them if you choose, but we recommend using only the pencil. The highlighter is great for one thing, highlighting, but it's not so hot when it comes to making notes, so if you choose to make use of the highlighter you'll need to use the pencil, too. It's true that highlighting a portion of the text makes it stand out a bit more compared to underlining it or circling it, saving a bit of time when you have to refer back to the passage. However, the small amount of time saved is almost certainly negated by the time lost by switching back and forth from the highlighter to the pencil. It's not a make or break decision, though, so if you feel it would be more efficient to use both the highlighter and the pencil, by all means do so. It's more important that you're relaxed and confident than that you save a few seconds here and there.

The Question Types

The questions you'll have to answer in the Reading Comprehension section will be complex and difficult, just like the passages themselves. Unlike reading comprehension tests you may have taken in the past, there won't be many questions for which only one answer choice will be clearly and inarguably the only possible correct answer. As the official LSAT Reading Comprehension instructions put it:

- *"more than one answer could conceivably be correct. However, you are to choose the best answer; that is, the response that most accurately and completely answers the question…"*

Don't make the mistake of thinking that "more than one" means "two." Sometimes you will encounter questions which have not just two, but several answer choices which could plausibly be correct. It's also a certainty that more than once you will be faced with questions which have two answer choices which seem to be saying almost exactly the same thing, and trying to understand the difference between them in order to choose "the best answer" will seem like an impossible task. Rest assured, however, that in each case only one answer will be acceptable. LSAT test writers spend a lot of time laboring over the precise wording of questions and answers in order to create this level of difficulty. Their purpose is to measure your ability to pick up on nuance and detail, an ability that will be crucial to your success in the legal field.

Fortunately, Reading Comprehension questions fall into a few basic types, which greatly simplifies the challenge you'll face on exam day. Knowing exactly what you'll be up against allows you to be much better prepared to do well on the exam. Here are the main kinds of questions you'll see on the Reading Comprehension test:

- What is the main point the author is making?/ What is the author's primary purpose in writing this?
- What is the author implying in this passage?/What can be inferred from this passage?
- Which of the following supports/weakens the author's argument?
- Based on the information in the passage, which of the following must be true?
- What does the author say about X in this passage?

Those are broad generalizations, of course – most questions won't be phrased exactly like any of the above, but approximately 75% of them will be some sort of variation on one of these themes. Here are some examples of the phrasing you'll see in the actual questions on the Reading Comprehension:

- Which one of the following most accurately expresses the main idea of the passage?
- Which one of the following would be the best title for this passage?
- Which of the following inferences is most strongly supported by this passage?
- The author implies which of the following in lines 17-19?
- Which of the following would most weaken the author's argument?
- The author's response to X would most likely be which of the following?
- In writing this, the author primarily seeks to…?
- Which one of the following most accurately and completely expresses the author's main point?

Most of the remaining questions will be about the author's tone, how the passage is structured, and definitions of words (which can be derived from information supplied in the passage).

Breaking Down the Questions

Let's take a deeper look at the main question types.

1) Main Point/Primary Purpose
Nearly every passage on the Reading Comprehension will have a question asking about what the author hopes to accomplish by writing this, or what her overriding point is. There is a lot of overlap between what the author's main point is and what the author's primary purpose is, so you can think of these two kinds of questions as essentially the same question, but expressed in a slightly different way. Basically, both of these questions boil down to this: "What message is the author trying to communicate?"

a) Main Point
Questions about the author's main point are not always phrased exactly alike, but are usually pretty straightforward. By this point in your academic career you should be familiar with this kind of question, as it's not only one of the most common ones on the LSAT Reading Comprehension exam, it's standard fare on any test of reading comprehension. By "straightforward" we don't mean to imply that these questions are easy to answer; we're only pointing out that the average test taker will have no trouble ascertaining the point of the question.

Almost all Reading Comprehension passages will contain a sentence that expresses the author's main point. Think of this sentence as the thesis statement of the passage. In a written essay, the thesis statement is almost always found in the last sentence of the first paragraph, but that won't be the case in these passages. You will sometimes find the thesis statement there, but many times you won't. The writers of these passages go out of their way to avoid falling into that kind of pattern, which is why formulaic approaches to the LSAT simply don't work. In fact, in some passages the thesis statement won't appear in the first paragraph at all, but one of the others.

The biggest difficulty test takers have with Main Point questions is that more than one of the answer choices might be an actual point made by the author, but not her main point. An incorrect answer choice might be a secondary point she made, or it could be one aspect of her main point, without accurately summing up the entire point. In many cases the main difference between a wrong choice and the right answer is that the incorrect one is too narrow, or too broad. Because of the phrasing and sentence construction of the answer choices, it's not always easy to distinguish these plausible sounding answer choices from the one that best encapsulates the main point. It's important to read all the choices carefully and deliberately before choosing an answer.

b) Primary Purpose
Every author has an overriding goal in mind when he writes; this is his primary purpose for writing the piece. His primary purpose can be any number of things. Here are a few possibilities:
- to provide information about a topic
- to demonstrate opposition to a person or thing
- to evaluate or examine a topic
- to challenge an idea, belief or practice
- to demonstrate support for a person or thing

- to convince someone of something
- to convert someone to a viewpoint or cause
- to critique or criticize something or someone
- to satirize or ridicule someone or something
- to clear up confusion about something
- to bring about change in some area

Those are just some of the primary purposes an author might have in mind when he sits down to write; obviously, there are many more. Unlike the main point of a passage, however, the primary purpose will rarely be stated overtly. You must be able to infer the author's primary reason for writing the passage even though it isn't spelled out. As they do with questions about the author's main point, LSAT writers specialize in surrounding the correct answer choice with others that are often remarkably similar to the actual answer. We can't stress enough how necessary it is to read all the answer choices before deciding that one is correct.

2) Implication/Inference

On the Reading Comprehension portion of the LSAT you will encounter many questions about what the author is implying in the passage, or what may be inferred from the passage. Just as is the case with the Main Point/Primary Purpose questions, they will be phrased in a variety of ways:
- With which of the following would the author most likely agree?
- The author implies which of the following?
- With which of the following would the author most likely disagree?
- It can be inferred from the passage that...
- Which of the following inferences is most strongly supported by the author's argument in paragraph two?
- In paragraph three, the author implies that his critics...
- The passage suggests which one of the following about X?
- The passage most strongly implies that the author agrees with which of the following statements?
- The passage provides evidence to suggest that the author would...

No matter how it is phrased, each implication/inference question is asking you about an idea or opinion that the author most likely believes in or subscribes to, even though he has not overtly said so in the passage. Sometimes the question will be about an implication/inference about a narrow sub-topic of the passage. If so, some of the answer choices will be quite similar with only slight differences between them. They can be so similar that a test taker in a hurry could easily fail to see any differences at all between them. Other questions will be broader, with each answer choice representing a clear and discrete alternative to the others. The latter are generally easier to answer than the former.

3) Supports/Weakens

For these questions, you'll be asked which of the answer choices most strengthens or weakens something the author says in the passage. The question could refer to one of the arguments the author makes, one of the conclusions he states, or even his main point. These questions will require you to consider the idea from the passage or the author's statement in light of information not mentioned in the passage, which would most strongly support or detract from the passage or statement. Their phrasing doesn't vary as much as some of the other question types:
- Which one of the following, if true, most supports the author's statement about X in paragraph three?

- Which one of the following, if true, most weakens the author's statement that...?
- Which one of the following, if true, most supports the author's conclusion?
- Which one of the following, if true, most weakens the author's suggestion that X is the best approach to...?

Notice that the correct answer is the one that *most* supports or weakens the statement or idea in question. Rest assured, one or more of the other answer choices will clearly support or detract from the statement or idea, but not quite as forcefully as the correct answer does. Also keep in mind that you will never have to decide if the new information being considered is correct or incorrect. These questions will always qualify the new information with the phrase "if true."

4) Must Be True/Cannot Be True
Must Be True questions are usually phrased along this line:
- Based on the information in the passage, which of the following must be true?
- Which of the following is most consistent with the author's conclusion that...?
- Based on the information in the passage, which of the following cannot be true?
- Which one of the following, if true, is LEAST consistent with the author's claim in paragraph 3?

These questions are the inverse of Supports/Weakens questions. Those questions ask you to assume that some new information is true, and then analyze the author's ideas or conclusions in light of it. On Must Be True questions, you'll be required to go in the other direction. You'll assume that the author's ideas or conclusions are true, and then you'll analyze some new information in light of the passage.

Must Be True questions are closely related to Implication/Inference questions. The main difference is that Implication/Inference questions revolve around the implicit but unwritten thoughts and beliefs of the author of the passage, while Must Be True questions are focused on asking you to use explicit/and or implicit information from the passage to evaluate new information. Again, you'll never need to be concerned about whether or not the information in the passage is actually true. In most cases a layman won't be qualified to make that determination. You'll answer these questions using the assumption that the information in the passage is reliable.

5) Explicit Information
These kinds of questions are the least subjective ones you will come across on the Reading Comprehension portion of the LSAT. Nearly every other Reading Comprehension question will require you to make an inference, interpretation or deduction of one sort or another in order to answer the question correctly. Questions about what the author is implying, what must be true based on the passage, how one thing relates to another, what would most weaken an author's argument, etc., all require you to make some sort of judgment call.

Explicit Information questions are different; there is no conjecture at all required to answer these questions. That is not to say that they're easy; on the contrary, they usually aren't much easier than the more subjective types of questions. Just as with the other question types, answer choices will be written in such a way that at least one of the incorrect choices (and probably more) will be similar enough to the correct one that careful thought will be required to choose the right answer. These questions can take several forms:
- the author lists each of the following drawbacks about the proposed canon revisions EXCEPT?

- the author states which one of the following about computers in the classroom?
- the passage provides information that answers which one of the following questions?
- according to the passage, some X have been mistakenly classified as which one of the following?
- the author states that admissions committees at top tier universities in America have which of the following characteristics?
- which one of the following is mentioned in the passage as an important factor in the development of?
- which one of the following describes a potential pitfall of embracing the new technology mentioned in paragraph four?

The Reading Comprehension portion of the LSAT is quite a challenge, and should not be underestimated. However, armed with the information in this guide, there's no reason to fear it. Study this until you're familiar with these main question types, and how to handle them. Then take the practice tests to ensure you're ready for the challenge on the day of the exam.

Analytical Reasoning Test

The Analytical Reasoning (or Games) section of the LSAT consists of approximately 24 questions, with a 35 minute time limit. Many people refer to this section as Logic Games, but that can be quite confusing, as the other reasoning section of the LSAT is called Logical Reasoning, so in this guide we'll use either Analytical Reasoning or Games. Although the other sections of the LSAT measure skills that are easily connected with doing well in law school, those measured in this section can be harder to pin down. Also, Analytical Reasoning is often considered to be the most time-challenging portion of the test, with only 35 minutes to complete 22 to 24 rather involved questions.

In the following sections, we will break down the question types found within this portion. First, however, it is worthwhile to briefly examine the format these problems will take on the LSAT.

The Analytical Reasoning section will contain four problems. Each problem will be followed by five, six, or seven questions. If you plan to try to answer them all, you will have a little over a minute to answer each of the questions.

Like problems in other sections, the Analytical Reasoning problems will test your ability to wade through a lot of information, think fast under pressure, and keep up the pace. On top of that, this section, more than any other, will require you to identify and keep a running tab on the relationships between different bits of information through various points of convergence. (On the other hand, this is the only part of the LSAT where a test taker can make absolutely sure that their answer is correct.)

Many examinees dread this section of the LSAT, with its requirement that you continually track a lot of information and relationships between the various bits of information. And there's no denying that it can be quite confusing. But one thing you will discover by practicing the problems in advance is that one or two of the Analytical Reasoning problem types will be easier for you to grasp and complete, relatively speaking, while others will be more difficult. Particularly since you will be testing under time-sensitive, high-pressure conditions, it is recommended that you first work out the problems that come more easily to you, and then go back around to complete those that take more time.

Also, if your experimental section turns out to be Analytical Reasoning, you will need to tackle both sections as if they were real, since you have no way of knowing which will one be scored and which one won't. But remember – you are not penalized for the number of wrong answers, so when time is short, guessing is a far better strategy than leaving questions blank.

There's no denying that for the vast majority of people the Analytical Reasoning section is by far the most difficult part of the LSAT. The material is itself extremely challenging, and, as if this weren't enough, the test designers intentionally include so many questions that it's nearly impossible to complete them all in a mere 35 minutes. Don't let this discourage you, though, because the Analytical Reasoning part of the LSAT is also the section where thorough preparation can make the biggest difference.

Of course, it's important to prepare for all three sections of the LSAT, but taking the time to learn how to understand and solve Analytical Reasoning games will be the easiest way for most people to significantly improve their score. That's because the other two sections measure skills people already use on a regular basis. It's certainly possible to improve a person's abilities at reading comprehension and/or logical reasoning, but most people taking the LSAT will already be fairly strong in these two areas. There is certainly upside potential there, but it's somewhat limited. The problems in Analytical Reasoning, however, require less commonly used skills, so the upside potential of mastering the skills needed to solve these kinds of problems is huge.

The *Real* Key to Success on the Analytical Reasoning Section

Out of all the powerful information in this guide, if you had to choose only one area to focus on, it should be the information in this section. It's that important.

In the Analytical Reasoning section of the LSAT the problems are in the form of what the LSAC calls *setups*. Each setup contains two main parts. The first is *elements* – these are sets of people (the most common), places, or things. The second is *conditions* – constraints under which the elements operate, which are limits on how they can be manipulated. Many people refer to the conditions as *rules* or *clues*; the three terms are interchangeable in this context. In order to answer the questions after the setup you will need to arrange, classify, group or otherwise manipulate the elements in accordance with the constraints.

Given that each setup will have several elements and various rules, some of which apply to all of the elements, and others which apply only to some of the elements, it will be virtually impossible to answer all 22-24 questions in the Analytical Reasoning section in the allotted 35 minutes by trying to figure the answers out in your head. In fact, trying to do so is probably the one thing that has the single biggest negative impact on the average person's LSAT score.

Trying to come up with the answers in your head will drag your score down in two ways. First, it's very unlikely that you'll be able to answer all the questions without guessing. You simply won't have time. Odds are high that you'll be forced to either leave a lot of the questions blank, or just take random guesses at them because you're running out of time. While wrong or blank answers won't lower your score in and of themselves, each one represents a question you could have answered correctly if you'd utilized a more effective strategy. In other words, while there's no penalty for an incorrect or missing answer, each one is a missed opportunity for raising your score.

Second, even in those cases where you spent a good bit of time thinking about the question, some of your answers are very likely to be wrong, because solving these problems mentally is extremely difficult. In fact, the key to success on the Analytical Reasoning section of the LSAT lies in understanding that it's not a pure reasoning test by any stretch of the imagination. **In actuality, your success on this section depends not just on your reasoning abilities, but also on your skill at quickly making accurate visual representations of complicated written information. In fact, the latter skill is probably even more important than the former**. In other words, Analytical Reasoning is just as much a diagramming test as it is a reasoning test, if not more so. Of course, LSAC can't come right out and call this section Rapid Diagramming, because that doesn't sound nearly as impressive (or nearly as intimidating) as Analytical Reasoning.

We said earlier that this is the only section where you can be 100% sure your answer is correct. That's because if you draw a diagram properly, you can simply look at your diagram and visually confirm the correct answer. We also said that even though the Analytical Reasoning section of the LSAT is the one that seems the most intimidating, it's also the section which offers the most room for improvement for raising your potential score. If you're like the average person, your skills at diagramming these kinds of problems are starting at what is essentially a baseline of zero. If you get only slightly good at diagramming Analytical Reasoning setups, you can expect a significant improvement in your potential LSAT score. If you take the time and effort to get very good at it, the impact on your score will be huge.

Not everyone who takes the LSAT is capable of achieving a high score. However, many people who actually are capable of ranking in the top percentiles of test-takers fail to do so, and wind up with a mediocre score – one that's nothing to brag about, and isn't good enough to get them into the best schools, let alone win them any scholarship money. For most of these aspiring lawyers, the main reason they didn't achieve the high score they were capable of is a poor performance on the Analytical Reasoning section.

> **When it comes to getting a high score on the LSAT, the single most important thing you can do between now and test day is to learn how to diagram these Analytical Reasoning setups quickly and effectively.**

The Fine Art of Diagramming

We're being facetious, of course - drawing diagrams for the LSAT is about as far away from being a fine art as it can get. So if you're not an artist, you can relax. No artistic ability is necessary in order to be able to draw effective diagrams for the Analytical Reasoning test. If you can draw a stick figure, you've got all the talent you need to create the simple diagrams which can mean the difference between failure and success on this portion of the LSAT. If you do happen to have some artistic ability, just check it at the door of the testing center. You'll want to keep your diagrams as simple and uncomplicated as possible. Doing so will not only reduce the time it takes to draw them, it will also mean you'll be able to come up with the correct answer more quickly. When it comes to Analytical Reasoning diagrams, less is definitely more.

Essentially, your diagrams will consist of three things: lines (including simple circles, boxes, and tables), symbols, and names of the elements from the setup. Once you've solved a question for a setup, you can keep the basic diagram for the rest of the questions for that setup, but you will sometimes have to erase most of the names and then rearrange them on the diagram for each question.

Now, you may be wondering how you'll be able to write out the names of five or more people, places or things, repeatedly, in the very limited time you'll have available. Well, you won't have to. Most of the time, you will be able to represent each element with only one letter – the initial of the name of the person, place or thing. In the vast majority of cases, the people who write the setups and questions for the LSAT make sure to never have two elements which begin with the same letter. In some cases, when the setups include the names of actual people (such as former Presidents) or days of the week, there may be two elements with the same first letter, but that can easily be dealt with by using the first two letters for those particular elements.

Rule Busters

Each problem provides you with some known information. These are the rules that you have to work with. Rule busters are choices that immediately clash with a rule and can be quickly ruled out.

Example:

John is sitting next to Bob.

This is a rule. Therefore any seating combination that does not have John sitting next to Bob is a rule buster, and is wrong. Quickly scan through the list of answer choices and eliminate all of those that have Bob and John sitting apart.

Example:

Mary is not sitting next to Bob.

Here is another rule. Quickly scan back through the answer choices and eliminate any that have Mary and Bob sitting together. For every rule that is given, quickly check and see if there are any answer choices that immediately bust the rule and eliminate them.

Symbols

Don't try to remember all of the information in your head. Sketch out the problem using the information provided. As much as possible, use symbols to represent the problem. Letters are great for abbreviation. Use *M* as a symbol for a man, and *W* as a symbol for a woman. Use the first letters in names to describe people. Therefore, John becomes *J* and Paul becomes *P*. If the problem involves a seating or standing arrangement, use blanks to represent the possible seats. Then if a rule states that John is in the rightmost seat, put a *J* in the rightmost blank. Fill in as much information as you can using your symbols. Symbols will help you save time from writing the names out and will allow you to make fast and accurate diagrams of the problem.

Scratch Paper

Use your text booklet as scratch paper extensively. It's a great ally! If you finish the Analytical Reasoning section without scribbles throughout, you didn't take advantage of all of your potential resources. A good diagram or drawing of the problem described is a huge aid when it comes to solving the problem.

Be forewarned though, when creating your drawings, you will need to be efficient. Don't waste time filling in more information that you need. This is why symbols are great tools. They will save time and effort. Don't include useless information on your diagram or spend time making it pretty. Fill in only what is clearly stated, or what you can quickly deduce. Focus on getting the bare essentials down on paper and spend your time more productively trying to solve the problem.

Tough Questions

If you are stumped on a problem or it appears too hard or too difficult, don't waste time. Move on. Remember though, if you can quickly check for obvious rule busters your chances of guessing correctly are greatly improved. Before you completely give up, at least check for the easy rule busters, which should knock out a couple of possible answers. Eliminate what you can and then guess at the remainder before moving on.

Face Value

Always accept the situation in the problem at face value. Don't read too much into it. The LSAT makers aren't trying to throw you off with a cheap trick. If the setup says there are six seats in a row, you can be confident that it is a single file row and one person is seated directly beside the next person and there are two ends to the row. Don't overcomplicate the problem by creating theoretical scenarios that will warp time or space. These are normal problems with solvable answers. It's just that all of the information isn't readily apparent and you have to figure things out.

Read Carefully

Understand what the problem is about. Read the description of the problem carefully. Don't miss the question because you misunderstood the description of the problem. The description is there because it is important in understanding the problem. Don't waste too much time though. You must read carefully and efficiently.

Loose vs Tight

Rules are often either loose or tight. Don't confuse the two when you check for rule breakers. A loose rule gives vague details about the problem. A tight rule gives specific details about the problem. Tight rules are much more helpful, because they provide more information, allowing you to make clear determinations about answer choices more easily.

Example:

> Loose: Bob is standing somewhere behind Joe.
> Tight: Bob is standing directly behind Joe.

Don't mistakenly eliminate an answer choice that has Bob standing two spaces back from Joe, if only the loose rule above is given. If the loose rule is given, you can only eliminate answer choices that have Bob in front of Joe.

Double Negatives

A double negative can be treated as an affirmative. If a rule or answer choice has two negatives, mentally switch it to a single positive.

Example:

> He is not going to not be there. = He is going to be there.

Answer Selection

Eliminate choices as soon as you realize they are wrong. But be careful. Make sure you consider all of the possible answer choices. Just because one appears right, doesn't mean that the next one won't be even better. Take a second to make sure that the other choices are not equally obvious. Don't make a hasty mistake. There are only two times that you should stop before considering other answer choices. The first is when you are absolutely positive that the answer choice you have selected satisfies all of the rules. The second is when time is almost out and you have to make a quick guess.

Don't worry if you are stuck between two answer choices that seem right. By eliminating the other three your odds of answering correctly are now 50/50. Rather than wasting too much time, play the odds. You are guessing, but guessing wisely, because you've been able to knock out some of the answer choices that you know are wrong. If you are eliminating choices and realize that the answer choice you are left with is also obviously wrong, don't panic. Start over and consider each choice again. There may easily be something that you missed the first time and will catch on the second pass.

Common Sense

When in doubt, use common sense. These problems will not require you to make huge leaps of logic. If you think a leap of logic is necessary, read back through question and the set of conditions in order to gain a better understanding. Don't read too much into the question or set of conditions. Use your common sense to interpret anything that isn't clear. These are normal problems rooted in reality.

Final Notes

Some problems may have complicated reasoning that must be sorted through. Before you pick an answer choice and work it out in great detail, which takes a lot of time, first look briefly through the other answer choices to see if any of them are readily obvious as being correct. Always use your time efficiently. Don't panic, and stay focused. Work systematically. Read the problem carefully. Eliminate the answer choices that are immediately wrong and are rule busters. Keep narrowing the search until you are either left with the answer or must guess at the answer from a more selective group of choices.

Analytical Reasoning Questions: Types

As soon as you look at the Analytical Reasoning section of the LSAT, you will immediately notice a difference in problem style and section structure. Not only are the skills tested a little bit different, but so is the way that testing occurs.

In order to approach the Analytical Reasoning section with confidence, it is important to first become familiar with the types of questions found here. There are four primary types of Analytical Reasoning (Games) questions. While some problems may combine types, the basic question types you will see are as follows:

1. **Ordering:** In this type of problem, the examinee must order the players of the question (and players may be human, animal, objects, or something else altogether) in a specific sequence based on the conditions provided.
2. **Selection:** The examinee must select a smaller group of players from within the larger group, based strictly upon the criteria given.
3. **Assignment:** For these problems, the examinee must assign players into different groups.
4. **Connection:** Given specific criteria or instructions, the examinee is asked to connect some of the players in a particular way.

Not only does the content of the question differ from that of other LSAT sections, but the layout of the problems does as well. Instead of showing you a short text followed by one or more questions, the Analytical Reasoning section will include condition statements as well as a passage. Normally, there will be an introductory statement to familiarize you with the players for the problem. As noted above, these players may belong to any species or type that the test preparers care to incorporate into their creatively worded problems.

The second condition statement will then establish the rules and conditions which you must follow for that problem set. It is rare for a question to change any conditions, but it is not unheard of, so be aware of that possibility. Another detail to keep in mind is that in the Games section, there is only one answer that can conceivably be correct. While other sections may require you to identify the *best* answer, meaning that at least one other answer choice might be partially correct, that's not the case with the Analytical Reasoning section. Answer choices in Games can't be partially correct; they're either right, or they're wrong, with no shades in between. So once you have identified a correct response, you are done with that question and need waste no more time on further analysis, because all other choices are completely wrong.

Analytical Reasoning Questions: Ordering Problems

Analytical Reasoning ordering problems naturally require the examinee to put the players (which could be anything) in a particular order based on the conditions given. The ordered sequence could be any type of configuration—not necessarily a list. With all of the possibilities available, it is certainly a good idea to become very familiar with the specifics of the conditions and instructions as set forth in the problem. Whatever can be definitively known from a careful reading of the conditions will lay the foundation for the questions that come after.

In terms of ordering problems found on the LSAT, you may be asked to do the following types of order-related tasks in Analytical Reasoning problems:
- Identify all of the positions an individual player may or may not occupy within the sequence.
- Decide which players may or may not be across from or next to one another in a given sequence.
- Identify the particular location of an individual player within the sequence.
- Calculate the number of positions separating two particular players within the sequence.
- Determine all players who must come before or after a particular player in a given sequence.

The following example will help illustrate the type of ordering tasks you may be asked to perform. Creating a diagram of the information provided will be helpful in answering these questions quickly and accurately:

> Team X has ten players—Joe, Carrie, Miguel, Alice, Walley, Hari, Kris, Damon, Pete, and Helen. During practice, they stand in a circle for passing exercises. The following is a description of the sequence of their drill:
>
> Miguel passes to Helen.
> Helen passes to Kris.
> Kris passes to Walley.
> Walley passes to Carrie.
> Carrie passes to Pete.
> Pete passes to Hari.
> Hari passes to Alice.
> Alice passes to Joe.
> Joe passes to Damon.
> Damon holds the ball.
>
> The first pass is made to the player directly across. Each subsequent pass must be made to a teammate four or five spaces removed from the passing player in an alternating sequence. No player may catch or pass more than once.

The problem is a simple one, but there is a lot of information to sort through and a lot of little pieces to put in order. It is easy to see why working it out in a drawing can be quite helpful in making sense of the problem. Consider, for example, how sketching the description would make the following questions very simple to answer:

1. Where does Damon stand in relation to Miguel?

or

2. Which players stand three removed from Carrie in the circle?

A diagram easily shows you that Miguel is standing right next to Damon; you might figure that one out strictly from a good read of the question. As for Carrie, both Helen and Damon stand three spaces removed from her – a connection that's more difficult to make without a diagram.

Analytical Reasoning Questions: Selection Problems

A universal must-do for the Analytical Reasoning section is careful attention to the conditions set out for the problem; selection problems are no exception. There are a number of facts you will pick up about each player within the conditions, as well as what each may or may not do, how they can and cannot be connected – in other words, strict parameters for how they operate. Selection problems require that you pay special attention to this information because you will be using it to pull smaller groups out of the main one.

Parameters for the problem may look something like this:
Amy must select three employees to go on the junket.

To reach a determination for questions like this, you will need to consider the following aspects:
- Who must be selected according to the conditions delineated
- Who is eligible for selection
- Who is not eligible for selection
- If certain specific players are selected, which other players must or must not be selected
- After considering the information, how many players are actually eligible

The following example will help to illustrate the above concepts:

There are six siblings who attend the same college. They are Naya, Chris, Maggie, Elliott, Joel, and Petra. Five classes are scheduled for the coming semester, which they may attend, subject to the following restrictions:

If Joel signs up for a particular class, then Petra does not sign up for the same class.
If Naya signs up for a particular class, then Chris does not sign up for the same class.
If Petra signs up for a particular class, then either Maggie or Elliott may sign up for the same class, but not both.
If Chris does not sign up for a particular class, then neither Maggie nor Petra may sign up for that class.

As you can see, there is a lot to keep track of, right from the beginning. You can see why drawing a diagram would be necessary to solve these problems. Diagrams make it easier to reference those connections in answering a series of questions for which each creates a slightly different group and can speed response time.

Considering the set of conditions above, try the following question:

If Naya enrolls for a particular class, what is the maximum number of other siblings who may also attend that class?

As you can see, drawing up the connections when you first read through the conditions can prevent you from having to waste precious time in reviewing the conditions for each additional question.

Analytical Reasoning Questions: Assignment Problems

At first glance, Analytical Reasoning assignment questions will look rather similar to selection questions. In both cases, you will be asked to select individuals out of a larger group based on the stated conditions. The primary difference is that in selection problems, you will identify players from the larger group and discard the rest for the purposes of that question. In assignment problems, however, you must select and assign *every* player identified into one group or another – there are no wallflowers in assignment problems.

The following comparison should serve to illustrate the difference:

Selection Problem

There are six siblings who attend the same college. They are Naya, Chris, Maggie, Elliott, Joel, and Petra. Five classes are scheduled for the coming semester, which they may attend, subject to the following restrictions: . . .

If Naya enrolls for a particular class, what is a complete list of those siblings who may also attend that class?

Assignment Problem

There are six siblings who attend the same college. They are Naya, Chris, Maggie, Elliott, Joel, and Petra. Two classes, the green class and the yellow class, are scheduled for the same weekdays and times. Each of the siblings must enroll in one of the two classes. All of the siblings mentioned above may attend, subject to the following conditions: . . .

Which of the siblings will enroll in the green class?

It should be immediately obvious that the primary difference between the two problems is that the assignment problem requires that every person be accounted for and assigned a slot in one group or the other. While the same skills used in selection problems can be used in solving assignment problems, many test takers find the assignment problems easier to solve. Because all players must be placed in a group, there are fewer loose ends. This makes it simpler for the examinee to account for everyone and ensure they have not missed something. For this reason, many people prefer assignment problems to selection problems, despite the additional step.

Question types that assignment problems may ask the examinee to address include:

1. Determine which players are required to be in a certain group.
2. Determine which players may be included in a certain group.
3. Determine the number of players to be grouped in a particular category.
4. Determine which players are not eligible for inclusion in a certain group.
5. Determine which players must or must not be paired with other particular players.

Analytical Reasoning Questions: Connection Games

Analytical Reasoning connection games problems are similar to assignment problems in that they require you to place each of the listed players into a group based on specified conditions. With connection games problems, however, you must do this based on connections or characteristics of the different players as delineated in the set conditions: you are *connecting* the players to those characteristics.

There is a lot going on, so it's good to start by breaking the problem down into smaller, more manageable parts. The following systematic progression works well in sorting out the problem prior to tackling the questions:

- Begin by listing out the various players. The players are often listed in a consecutive string, which makes this fairly simple.
- Identify and make note of the different characteristics possible for the various players.
- Where possible, match the different characteristics to specific players. Sometimes possible characteristics are listed in the negative (in an attempt to befuddle LSAT examinees). For instance, it could be phrased similarly to this: all players who have Characteristic Y cannot have Characteristic Z.

Consider the following example and practice applying the above steps:

There are four students: Anna, Brandon, Charles, and Donita. These students dislike the following classes: algebra, biology, and P.E., consistent with the following:

Each student dislikes at least one of the classes;
No student dislikes all three classes;
At least two, but not all four, of the students dislike biology;
If Brandon dislikes a class, then Donita also dislikes that class;
If a student does not like biology, then that student also dislikes algebra;
Charles does not like algebra.

From reviewing the above example, it is easy to see how you could get your wires crossed as you go deeper into the questions (which can build on one another).

So to apply the above steps, we first list out the players: Anna, Brandon, Charles, and Donita. Next, you make note of the various characteristics, which are, in this case, the classes the students do not like. Note the characteristics that are directly attributed to a particular player (Charles does not like algebra), as well as those that are indirectly attributed to a player (if Brandon dislikes a class, then so does Donita).

Once you have done this, you are prepared to face the types of questions that will be attached to the connection games problems, such as:

1. Determine which players must have a particular characteristic.
2. Determine which players could have a particular characteristic.
3. Determine which players definitely could not be connected to a particular characteristic.
4. Separate out which players must, must not, or could possibly be connected to the same characteristics as other players.

Skipping Problems: Some Advice

Because of the difficulty level encountered in Analytical Reasoning, some test takers make a strategic decision to skip some of the problems in this section of the LSAT in order to have more time to concentrate on a lower number of questions, hopefully maximizing the number of questions they answer correctly. This is a common strategy, and given how the LSAT is scored, and the severe time constraints of the Analytical Reasoning section, it can make a lot of sense to follow it. In other words, since you don't have enough time to give all the questions the attention needed to answer them, and since the LSAT score is based only on correct answers, it's quite logical to devote more time to a lower number of questions if it leads to you answering more questions correctly.

If you decide to employ this strategy, it's important for you to know that not all the Analytical Reasoning questions on the LSAT are of equal difficulty. All of them are difficult, of course, but some are less difficult than others, while some are more difficult. So which ones should you skip, and which ones should you focus on? Well, while some people would disagree, most test takers find that assigning setups are the hardest, ordering setups are the least difficult, and grouping setups fall somewhere in between. Also, you should not skip the first setup, as it is never the hardest one on the exam.

Another important consideration is that, generally speaking, setups which have more conditions are usually easier to answer than those with fewer rules. It may seem that the opposite would be true. This is probably due to the fact that reading and grasping more rules takes more time than does reading and grasping fewer rules. They say that appearances are often deceptive, and in this case they're right. It's not reading and grasping the rules that will take up most of your time on the Analytical Reasoning section; it's thinking about how to come up with the correct answer. The more information you have to start with, the fewer things you have to figure out in order to determine the right answer. So, when it comes to solving problems quickly, the more conditions, the better.

Logical Reasoning Test

The Logical Reasoning (LR) section of the LSAT consists of two 35 minute exams with approximately 25 questions each. It's the part of the LSAT that most directly tests the skills you will use as a lawyer—comprehending and analyzing an argument and poking holes in it or, if it's valid, following the argument to its logical conclusion. When it comes to your LSAT score, *Logical Reasoning is twice as important as any other portion of the test*, because of the fact that the LSAT includes two LR sections, as opposed to only one 35 minute test for Reading Comprehension or Analytical Reasoning. So, even if you shine on the other sections, it is impossible to get a high score on the LSAT without doing well in Logical Reasoning.

Because of its importance and complexity, we will spend a lot of time discussing study tips for Logical Reasoning. We will break down the basic concepts, question types, underlying suppositions, issues, types of arguments and argumentation patterns, what distinguishes a weak argument from a strong one, and more, showing you how to logically take apart the argument piece-by-piece to determine the correct answer.

Throughout the Logical Reasoning section, keep the following general information in mind:
- There are 24-26 questions in each Logical Reasoning section; on most LSAT versions there are a total of 50-52 Logical Reasoning questions.
- The time factor in Logical Reasoning is not the same as in the Analytical Reasoning section, which is deliberately designed to make it extremely difficult to answer all the questions in the allotted time. The creators of the LSAT believe 35 minutes allows the average test taker enough time to complete the 24-26 questions on each Logical Reasoning exam, so it's best to start with the first question and work your way through.
- Your score depends on the number of correct answers—not the number of wrong ones—so you are not penalized for guessing.
- *You are not trying to determine whether the argument itself is correct, only whether or not it is logical.* That means that sometimes the correct answer to a question will contain a statement or information that is not actually true in the real word. As counterintuitive as it may seem, comprehending the relationship between the different facts and assumptions leading to that answer is more important than the objective accuracy of an argument or answer choice. Answer using only the information provided in the question. The opposite is also true – sometimes an *incorrect* answer choice will contain information that's true in the real world.
- Assuming you have studied the various types of arguments used for the Logical Reasoning section, the best approach is to begin by determining which type of question you are looking at. Accurately identifying the question type will be a big help in sorting correct answers from incorrect ones.

What's in the Logical Reasoning Section?

Just as in the Reading Comprehension portion of the LSAT, you'll be dealing with reading passages in the Logical Reasoning section. Don't worry, though; they aren't nearly as long or complex as the Reading Comprehension passages. Many will be under 10 lines long, virtually all of them will have less than a dozen lines, and you will usually encounter several that consist of no more than four or five lines. The passage itself is known as the **stimulus**, and is followed by a question. You may have seen the term **question stem** used in discussions of the LSAT, particularly in reference to the

Logical Reasoning or Analytical Reasoning sections, and wondered what it means. Well, it just means the question itself, not including the answer choices. For simplicity's sake, we'll usually just refer to it as the **question** in this guide.

Sometimes the stimulus will be nothing more than a presentation of some different facts, but in most cases, it will contain an **argument**. Most people think of an argument as a verbal or written conflict between two people, some sort of heated dispute. Two strangers at a bar screaming at each other about politics would be said to be having an argument. However, that is not the meaning of the word in the world of logic and philosophy. On the LSAT, an argument is basically an attempt to persuade by presenting evidence. In an argument on the LSAT, the author states his case.

You will encounter all kinds of arguments on the exam. An argument may be logically flawed, or it may be perfectly logical. It may be weak or strong. Your task on this portion of the LSAT will be to rapidly and accurately comprehend the argument, and then analyze it in some way based on the criteria in the question. In some cases, you won't have much trouble doing so, but for most of the questions you'll have to do some serious reasoning to get to the right answer.

If the stimulus contains an argument, then no matter what kind of argument it is, it will consist of two basic elements – the **premise(s)**, and the **conclusion**. The conclusion is the point the author is trying to convince the reader of, while the premises constitute the evidence he provides to support his conclusion. In other words, an author's conclusion is the *what* of his argument, and the premises are the *why*. Here's an example of a short, concise argument:

Alice has a 4.0 GPA and she scored in the 99th percentile on the Medical College Admission Test, so she is certain to be admitted to an elite medical school.

The conclusion is that Alice should have no worries about being accepted by an elite medical school. The premises are that she has a 4.0 GPA and that her MCAT score is in the 99th percentile. Now, as we said, this is a very basic argument, so let's add some additional information:

Alice has a 4.0 GPA and she scored in the 99th percentile on the Medical College Admission Test, so she is certain to be admitted to an elite medical school. With her work and study habits she will be at the top of her class. When she graduates, she'll have her pick of residencies thanks to her prestigious degree and record. Obviously, Alice is going to have a hugely successful career in medicine.

This changes things quite a bit. The new argument, while not highly complex, is definitely more complex than the one in the first passage. Notice that the point the author was trying to express in the first passage is no longer his conclusion. His new conclusion is that Alice is going to have a very successful medical career. What happened to his previous conclusion? It has now become a **sub-conclusion**, which helps build the case for his actual conclusion. You will run into this kind of argument several times on the LSAT. It's important to be able to distinguish a sub-conclusion from a conclusion, so you must read carefully. Also, there's no rule in logic that says a conclusion must come at the end of the argument. Look at how we can rearrange this argument:

Alice is going to have a hugely successful career in medicine. She has a 4.0 GPA and she scored in the 99th percentile on the Medical College Admission Test, so she is certain to be admitted to an elite medical school. With her work and study habits she will be at the top of her class. When she graduates, she'll have her pick of residencies thanks to her prestigious degree and record.

This is making the very same argument as before, only worded differently. The conclusion is now in the first sentence, appearing before the sub-conclusion. So always keep in mind that the conclusion can appear anywhere in an argument. Furthermore, there can also be more than one sub-conclusion. Careful reading is just as critical on the Logical Reasoning portion of the LSAT as it is on the other sections.

Logical Reasoning Strategies and Tips

Here are some brief tips and guidelines for helping you do your best on this section:

<u>Do NOT Read the Question First</u>

You need to decide on a consistent strategy for attacking each Logical Reasoning problem long before you ever walk into the testing center. In fact, you should do this before you even begin taking practice tests. So what's the best strategy? *Our strong recommendation is that you should always read the argument before reading the question.* It's important to note that this is the same approach we recommend you employ on the Reading Comprehension section of the LSAT. In fact, we say that one of the worst things you can do on the Reading Comprehension portion is to read the questions first and the passage second, even though this is a popular strategy. The same holds true for the Logical Reasoning section of the LSAT. Reading the question first will often cause you to be distracted or confused while you're reading the argument, and in almost all cases, you'll wind up having to read the question again anyway, wasting a lot of valuable time. Don't try to read the question first, and then the argument. You'll only slow yourself down, making it even harder to complete all of the questions in the very brief thirty-five minutes.

<u>Opposites</u>

Often, when two answer choices are a pair of direct opposites, one of them is correct. The paragraph or passage will often contain established relationships (e.g., when this goes up, that goes down). The question may ask you to draw conclusions from this and will give two similar answer choices that are opposites.

Example:
  1) *If other factors are held constant, then increasing the interest rate will lead to a **decrease** in housing starts*
  2) *If other factors are held constant, then increasing the interest rate will lead to an **increase** in housing starts*

Once you realize there are two answer choices which are opposites, you should examine them closely. One of the two is likely to be the correct answer. Of course, they often won't be as easy to spot as the two answer choices in this example. In many cases the wording of the two choices won't be nearly as similar to each other as is the case above. However, it's the meanings that are important, not the particular phrasing.

Watch Out for Red Herrings

Are you familiar with the term *red herring*? It's a literary device used by writers to mislead people into drawing a wrong conclusion about something or someone in the story. Novelists and scriptwriters often employ this device. For example, in a murder mystery, the dead man's butler may be subtly portrayed as scheming and greedy, leading many readers to conclude that he committed the murder. In the end, however, the grieving widow is revealed to be the actual culprit, the butler's putative greed and deceit notwithstanding.

Well, novelists and scriptwriters aren't the only people who regularly use red herrings in their line of work; so do the folks at the Law School Admission Council, who are responsible for creating the LSAT. In fact, creating red herrings is a huge part of their job. The designers of the exam deliberately create wrong answer choices that are very close to being correct. One of the most important duties of their job is to go to great lengths to attempt to convince you to choose the wrong answer, and, obviously, they wouldn't be very successful if none of the incorrect answer choices sounded plausible. If that were the case, all you would have to do would be go down the list and eliminate the four choices that are clearly implausible, and the only one left would be the correct answer. That kind of exam wouldn't be much of a challenge, obviously.

However, on most Logical Reasoning questions there will be three answer choices that aren't all that close to being correct, and only one that could really trip you up. That's because there simply aren't very many ways of coming up with an answer choice that sounds *almost* right, but isn't. An answer that's almost right but *not quite* has to strike the test taker as extremely plausible, and that makes it very difficult to create wrong answers that appear to be correct. So, for the most part, you should have no trouble picking out the blatantly incorrect answers. Once you've eliminated the obviously wrong answers, then you only have to choose between two possibilities. That's the good news. The bad news is that while eliminating three answer choices may make it a bit simpler to select the correct answer, it certainly doesn't make it a snap, because you'll now have to decide which of the two remaining answers is correct, and which one is an artfully constructed red herring.

There are several kinds of red herrings. Here are some that LSAT designers employ most often.

1. Taking Things to an Extreme

In many arguments, the LSAT writers will include an answer choice that takes a point made in the passage to an unjustified extreme. Consider this passage:

Many so-called conservatives are eager to have America go to war, while at the same time they condemn President Jones for running up massive federal deficits. This makes no sense. One of the historic foundational principles of conservatism is opposition to deficit spending on the part of the government. Well, President Jones is not to blame for these huge budget deficits; they are actually the fault of his allegedly conservative predecessor, President Smith, who hastily started a long and very expensive war without first exhausting all other options.

Given the statement above, which of the following must be true?

President Jones is not a conservative

The author of the passage is a liberal

President Smith was a Republican

People who are true conservatives should not be eager to go to war, because wars lead to budget deficits.

Many people calling themselves conservative think going to war is more important than having a balanced budget.

As we mentioned earlier, on most arguments you should expect to find three answer choices that you can quickly dismiss. Let's look at each answer, starting with A. If the argument is correct, must it also be true that President Jones is not a conservative? No, not at all. We know that many professing conservatives are condemning Jones for the large deficits, but that doesn't mean that Jones is a liberal or a moderate. Many political partisans are more strident about condemning politicians of their own persuasion who fail to please them than they are about condemning politicians in other camps. Thus, there is absolutely nothing in the passage that means it must be true that President Jones is not a conservative. Therefore, A is out.

How about B, then – is it necessarily true that the author of the passage is a liberal? Again, the answer is no. There is nothing in the passage that requires us to draw the conclusion that the author is a liberal. He might well be, but he could also be a frustrated conservative. For that matter, he could be a moderate, or even an apolitical person, and this argument could be part of a larger "a pox on both their houses" article. So, B is easily dismissed.

Moving on to C, does it logically follow from the passage that the former president was a Republican? No, it does not. Now, of the three answers which are obviously wrong, this is the one that would be most likely to trip a few people up due to careless reading, and mentally bringing in real world facts to solve the problem. We know from the passage that President Smith was allegedly conservative. However, we know nothing of his party affiliation. While in the real world of American politics most people rightfully associate the label conservative with the Republican Party, that doesn't mean that there aren't some Democrats who call themselves conservatives. In fact, in the 1992 election, Bill Clinton and Al Gore won by selling themselves as conservative Democrats, in contrast to liberals such as Michael Dukakis and Walter Mondale. So, conservative does not have to mean Republican. Furthermore, the passage doesn't mention Republicans or Democrats at all. It could be describing a hypothetical future America in which neither party exists any longer. Thus, C is incorrect, too, and obviously so.

So, we have two answers left to choose from. Is D the right choice? Can we conclude from the passage that wars lead to budget deficits? Many people would select this answer. Would you? You should not, as the reasoning is faulty. In fact, it's a great example of how LSAT designers trip people up. Let's look at it more closely.

In this red herring, the test designers take a specific point, but then make far too much of it of it. They start with an inarguable fact from the passage – the author stated that President Jones shouldn't be blamed for the huge federal budget deficits during his tenure; the blame should actually be assigned to the man he succeeded, President Smith, who started an expensive war while he was in the White House. This is a perfectly reasonable argument because wars usually *are* very expensive, and in the recent history of America, they have certainly led to massive deficit spending. Also, for the purposes of the LSAT, we should assume the truth of the facts presented in an argument, unless instructed otherwise.

Furthermore, most conservatives favor fiscal restraint and generally oppose running up deficits. So, a very good case can be made that people who are true conservatives should have opposed President Smith's getting America into an expensive war before all other options had failed.

However, answer choice D goes much further than that. It says that *wars lead to budget deficits*. It doesn't say that wars *tend to* result in budget deficits, or that *most* wars in history have led to deficit spending. It makes a categorical statement that wars result in budget deficits. This is an If/Then statement. Remember, If/Then statements rarely appear on the Logical Reasoning exam in their pure form. They are usually implied. In this sentence, the phrase *because wars lead to budget deficits* contains this implied If/Then statement:

If a country goes to war, then it will experience budget deficits.

However, this does not logically follow from the information we have in the passage. There's nothing in the passage that tells us that all wars in history have caused budget deficits, or that all wars in the future will do so, let alone that war always leads to budget deficits. All we know from the passage is that huge federal deficits under President Jones followed a war started by President Smith. Does this mean that all wars, everywhere, at all times, lead to budget deficits? Is it possible to imagine a scenario where a country goes to war and doesn't experience budget deficits as a result?

Couldn't the government of a country conceivably fund a war without running up deficits by using budget surpluses left over from previous years, or by raising taxes, or a combination of both? Yes, it could. Isn't it also possible that if Nation A goes to war with Nation B, Nation B could surrender almost immediately, resulting in a very short and very inexpensive war, the cost of which could be entirely covered by Nation A's current military budget? Yes, that's certainly a possibility, too.

So, based on the information in the passage, we cannot say categorically that wars lead to budget deficits. The fact that President Smith's wars resulted in budget deficits does not mean that all wars *must* have that same effect. Therefore, D is incorrect, even though it seems to make sense. It's wrong because it goes to an extreme, by taking one occurrence of something and making it into a hard and fast rule.

Notice that this tactic of going to extremes works in the opposite direction, too. Instead of making a leap from something happening *in one case* to a rule about it happening *in every case*, the answer choice could just as easily call for the illogical conclusion that because something *didn't happen* in a specific case it *never happens* in any cases.

Watch carefully for categorical words in arguments and answer choices, such as *always, all, must, never, none, can't, only, absolutely, certainly*, etc. If one of these words shows up in an answer choice, it's usually incorrect, unless the argument also makes a similar categorical claim, either expressed or implied. If one of these kinds of words appears in the argument itself, then look for an answer choice that aligns with it.

Keep in mind, however, that a categorical statement can exist without using any of these tipoff words. In the example above, the word *all* doesn't appear in the critical phrase *because wars lead to budget deficits.* It is clearly implied, however, because there are no modifiers such as *some* or *most* in the phrase that would limit the statement as applying only to a number of wars less than all.

The correct answer is E. Notice that it uses the word *many* as a modifier, just as the author does, and doesn't make a blanket statement about all conservatives. If we assume the argument is true, that means that the first sentence of the argument must be true, which logically leads to the conclusion found in E.

2. Irrelevancy | Similar Language | Parallel Reasoning

You'll run across many answer choices that seem to be correct, but which are actually completely irrelevant to the argument.

You'll also find answer choices that attempt to trip you up by using language that is similar to some of the language used in the passage.

You will also come across incorrect answers which seem right because they employ parallel reasoning.

Sometimes you'll encounter answers that combine two or more red herrings. Here's an example combining Irrelevancy, Similar Language, and Parallel Reasoning.

Let's return to the same argument, but change it up a little at the end:

> Many so-called conservatives seem eager to have America go to war, while at the same time they condemn President Jones for running up massive federal deficits. This makes no sense. One of the historic foundational principles of conservatism is opposition to deficit spending on the part of the government. Well, President Jones is not to blame for these huge budget deficits; they are actually the fault of his allegedly conservative predecessor, President Smith, who hastily started a long and very expensive war without first exhausting all other options. So-called conservatives who support rushing into war are not real conservatives.

Now, suppose the question was:

Which of the following, if true, would most strengthen the argument?

And suppose this was one of the answer choices:

Historically, conservatives have strongly condemned homosexuality, but today many so-called conservatives actually support the legalization of same-sex marriage.

Would this statement strengthen the argument? At first glance, it might seem to. The fact that people who support same-sex marriage would not have been regarded as conservatives in past generations certainly seems to go along with what the author is saying. Didn't he assert that many self-proclaimed conservatives have moved away from their foundational principles? If conservatives used to strongly oppose homosexuality, but today many conservatives approve of same-sex marriage, isn't that evidence that many of today's self-proclaimed conservatives aren't true conservatives, strengthening the author's argument? Many people would select this answer choice.

However, the author's argument isn't that many self-proclaimed conservatives aren't true conservatives because they have moved away from *some* foundational principles. He only mentions one foundational principle of conservatism – opposition to deficit spending, and that is the only standard he employs for determining if someone is a true conservative. Here is his argument in syllogism form:

The recent war led to budget deficits.

- 52 -

True conservatives oppose budget deficits.

Anyone who is eager to go to war is not a true conservative.

The author's argument is very narrowly focused, and does not address any other aspect of conservatism besides opposition to deficit spending. We have no idea if he believes that self-described conservatives have moved away from any other foundational principles of conservatism, or if he even believes that opposition to homosexuality is a foundational principle of conservatism. So, this answer choice doesn't strengthen the author's argument at all. What conservatives believe now or used to believe about homosexuality or same-sex marriage has absolutely no bearing on the author's argument, which is that anyone who is eager to go to war is not a true conservative. This answer choice not only fails to strengthen the argument, it is completely irrelevant. Nonetheless, it would fool many test takers.

Why is this answer choice so deceptive? Why is it that many people would think it strengthens the author's argument when, in actuality, it's completely irrelevant? There are several reasons this answer would fool many test takers. First, it's factually true – nearly all conservatives of past generations regarded homosexuality as extremely immoral, but these days many reject that view, and even endorse same-sex marriage. This is enough by itself to trick many examinees into choosing this answer.

We can't stress enough that you must not take real world factual accuracy into consideration at all on this portion of the LSAT; you must think of yourself as being in a self-contained universe while you answer questions on the Logical Reasoning section of the exam. Ignore everything outside of that universe, because the only facts that matter are the ones you're dealing with on the test, and some of them would be wrong in the real world. You must constantly be on guard against this tendency to work factual accuracy into the answer selection process, because it's very easy to fall into it without even realizing it.

Another reason the answer choice is so deceptive is that it uses some of the same language the author uses when it mentions *self-proclaimed conservatives*. This is the exact same phrasing that the author of the passage uses in the first sentence. Many test takers would not even catch this, but their brains would nonetheless make a connection between this answer and the argument without realizing it, simply because it uses the same phrasing.

Furthermore, the phrasing is pejorative, as *so-called* is used only to describe someone we don't regard as authentic, as the real deal. No one would use the phrase so-called expert to describe someone they regard as a real expert. Using this phrasing, both the passage and the answer choice convey the idea that there are a lot of phony conservatives running around out there. Because our minds look for reasons to make connections, and because when there's one connection there are often more, it's easy to mistakenly conclude that since the answer choice supports the author's view that many people calling themselves conservatives are no such thing, it also supports his main argument. (Again, this would not necessarily be a conscious thought process.)

Finally, the wrong answer employs parallel reasoning. Both the answer and the passage say that many people calling themselves conservatives aren't actual conservatives, and they both do so based on what the writer sees as a failure or refusal on the part of these people to measure up to a certain standard, by not taking a position that all (or nearly all) conservatives used to take. Because our brain is constantly looking for patterns and connections, and because these two arguments are so similar in their logic, many people will conclude that the answer choice strongly supports the passage, but that's not true. It is a similar argument in its form, but it does nothing to strengthen the author's conclusion.

Benchmark
After you read the first answer choice, decide if it sounds correct or not. If it doesn't, move on to the next answer choice. If it does, make a mental note of it. This doesn't mean that you've definitely selected it as your answer choice; it just means that it's the best you've seen thus far. Go ahead and read the next choice. If the next choice is worse than the one you've already selected, keep going to the next answer choice. If the next choice is better than the choice you've already selected, make it your tentative answer. Repeat this process until you've gone through all five answer choices.
The first answer choice that you select becomes your standard. Every other answer choice must be benchmarked against that standard. That choice is correct until proven otherwise by another answer choice beating it out. Once you've decided that no other answer choice seems as good, do one final check to ensure that it answers the question posed.

New Information
Correct answers will usually contain only information contained in the paragraph and/or question. Rarely will completely new information be inserted into a correct answer choice. Occasionally the new information may be related in a manner that LSAT is asking for you to interpret, but this is rare.

Example:
   The argument above is dependent upon which of the following assumptions?

   A. Scientists have used Charles's Law to interpret the relationship.

If Charles's Law is not mentioned at all in the referenced paragraph and argument, then it is very unlikely that this choice is correct. All of the information needed to answer the question is provided for you, and so you should not have to make guesses that are unsupported or select answer choices that refer to unknown information that cannot be analyzed.

Logical Reasoning Basic Concept #1: Conditions

Both Logical Reasoning exams on the LSAT contain a variety of problem types, each with its own nuance and ideal solution strategy. Even so, a thorough comprehension of certain foundational concepts will make it much easier to correctly answer the questions regardless of the argument type.

The first foundational concept involves understanding how LSAT test writers make use of two types of conditions: **necessary conditions** and **sufficient conditions**. You'll need an understanding of these two concepts, and the differences between them, in order to do well in Logical Reasoning.

Necessary conditions are those that *must* be present in order for a certain outcome to occur. For instance, in order for a forest to catch fire and burn down, there must be an ignition source. So an ignition source is a necessary condition for a forest fire. A necessary condition is anything that's absolutely required to be present in order for something else to be present. In other words, if B can't exist unless A, then A is a necessary condition for B. Here's another example of a necessary condition:

All pregnant people are females.

Since a person cannot be pregnant without being a female, being a female is a necessary condition for being pregnant.

On the other hand, a sufficient condition is enough to bring about an outcome, but is not the only condition that can do so. Returning to the case of forest fires, for example, lightning strikes can cause forest fires. So, a lightning strike is enough, in and of itself, to cause a forest fire. It's not a necessary condition, however, because it's not the only way a forest fire can be started. So, while a lightning strike is not a necessary condition of a forest fire, it is a sufficient condition.

Going back to our second example, is being a female a sufficient condition for being pregnant? No; because other conditions must also be present, such as having undergone puberty, having been inseminated, etc. So, while being a female is a necessary condition for being pregnant, it is not a sufficient condition.

Of course, on the actual Logical Reasoning exam, few conditional statements will be expressed as clearly and succinctly as our example statement about being pregnant. In most cases there won't be a sentence that directly states *all members of A are members of B*, or something similar. In fact, there probably won't be any part of the argument that makes any kind of direct conditional statement. If an argument contains a conditional statement, it will usually be implied, meaning you'll have to reason it out for yourself. The arguments that have conditional statements, whether expressed or implied, will include them as part of a larger passage. You will need to ignore the noise, or the nonessential details of the passage, so you can distill the argument (or the answer choice) down to its essence in order to find the underlying conditional statement.

If/Then Statements

Conditional statements can be easily understood and analyzed when put into If/Then form. Doing so can also help you spot logical fallacies, which is what the Logical Reasoning exam is all about. Here's an example of an If/Then statement.

If it's raining, then Mr. Jones will be indoors.

The first part of the statement (the If part), is called the hypothesis. The second part (the Then part) is called the conclusion.

The statement is straightforward and uncomplicated. It's easy to understand, and hardly anyone would have any trouble with it. Things can get tricky, however, when we change some of the elements up. For example:

If Mr. Jones is indoors, then it's raining.

This is the *converse* of the original statement. But does it logically follow from the original statement? In other words, can we reason logically from the first statement and come up with this statement? No, we cannot. There could be any number of reasons Mr. Jones is indoors. He may be ill. He may be sleeping. He may be surfing the internet. We cannot say with certainty that, based on the original statement, because Mr. Jones is indoors it must be raining. It does not say that rain is the only condition which causes Mr. Jones to stay indoors. In other words, rain is a sufficient condition for Mr. Jones to be indoors, but it's not a necessary condition. *The converse of a conditional statement may or may not be true.*

Now let's look at the *inverse* of the original statement:

If it's not raining, then Mr. Jones will not be indoors.

Once again, the question we need to answer is this – does this logically follow from the initial conditional statement? No, it does not. Just as with the converse, there are a multitude of reasons Mr. Jones might be indoors. If this inverse conditional statement were true, then Mr. Jones would be required to be outside any time it's not raining, no matter what time it is, or what activity he's engaged in. *The inverse of a conditional statement may or may not be true.*

Now, let's look at one more change to the elements of the statement.

If Mr. Jones is not indoors, then it's not raining.

This is the *contrapositive* of the original conditional statement. Does it logically follow from it? Yes, it does. If Mr. Jones is indoors every time it's raining, then if he is not indoors it cannot be raining. *The contrapositive of a conditional statement is always true.*

Now, when we say that the inverse and converse of a conditional statement may or may not be true, and that the contrapositive of a conditional statement is always true, we're using *true* in the sense that you'll need to understand it for the Logical Reasoning exam. Obviously, it's hard to believe that there could actually be a person alive who has never been caught in the rain, and for the rest of his life will never be outside when it's raining. We're simply taking for granted that the conditional statement itself is true, so when we say that the contrapositive is true, we mean that it logically follows from the conditional statement.

We're not at all concerned with the real life factual accuracy of a statement, nor should you be when you take the LSAT. *Do not fall into the trap of measuring Logical Reasoning arguments by their factual accuracy.* You must judge them only on their logical consistency. Forget the real world when you sit down for the LSAT. Don't underestimate your tendency to go into fact-based mode. It's easy to think you won't fall into this trap, but we're so used to fact-based exams that it's very difficult for some people to avoid falling back on their experience and knowledge on the Logical Reasoning exam.

Logical Reasoning Basic Concept #2: Reasonableness

Not all arguments on the Logical Reasoning exam will involve If/Then statements. In many cases, you will need to evaluate an argument on the basis of how reasonable it is. That is, you will need to ask yourself if the conclusion makes sense based on the evidence presented. Or is the author making an untenable argument, because he didn't present sufficient evidence to support his conclusion? This represents much of what you'll be doing on the Logical Reasoning portion of the LSAT.

This is what juries in criminal trials do, of course. A prosecutor makes a case against a defendant, and the jury weighs the evidence she presents. If they believe that the evidence is strong enough that there can be no reasonable doubt that the defendant committed the act, they find him guilty. In most *civil* trials, though, the burden of proof is not as heavy – there only needs to be a preponderance of evidence in order to assign liability. In other words, in a civil trial the plaintiff only has to present evidence that indicates that it's more likely than not that the other party committed the act he's accused of.

On the other end of the scale, we all run across people making completely unwarranted leaps of logic on a regular basis, especially while we're surfing the internet or watching cable news talk shows. In those environments it's common to see people making outlandish claims based on very little evidence, or none at all:

The federal government's response to Hurricane Katrina proves that George Bush is a racist who hates black people.

Anyone who supports raising the minimum wage is a Communist who wants to destroy the American way of life.

Of course, most of the arguments we encounter on a daily basis fall somewhere in the middle of the two extremes of beyond a reasonable doubt, and utterly nonsensical. Consider this:

Jenny said the new Italian café is fantastic. We should go there for lunch tomorrow.

Many people would not consider that to be an argument, but it actually is. Your friend has reached a conclusion (we should eat lunch at the new restaurant tomorrow) and is trying to convince you that his conclusion is correct by presenting the evidence he bases it on (Jenny raved about the place). Is this a reasonable argument? That depends on a lot of different factors. How long have you known Jenny? Do you trust her judgment when it comes to food and restaurants? How much does she know about Italian food? Does her cousin own the Italian café? Is the speaker telling the truth about what Jenny said?

If you trust the person who told you this, and you think Jenny has a good track record when it comes to restaurant recommendations, then this argument would probably strike you as quite reasonable. The fact that Jenny vouched for the place would be enough evidence for you to agree with your friend's conclusion that you should have lunch there tomorrow.

Now, consider this argument:

Jenny knows good food, and she loves that Mexican restaurant on 23rd street that's for sale. We should buy it and franchise it.

Is this a reasonable argument? In other words, has your friend presented enough evidence to support his conclusion? Even if Jenny is something of a connoisseur, is the fact that she likes the food at a restaurant sufficient evidence for agreeing that putting tens of thousands of dollars (or more) into an extremely risky business venture is a good idea? No, not really. Now, the idea behind the argument is not completely illogical – after all, people generally buy or start a business in hopes of making a lot of money, popular restaurants tend to make a lot of money, good food is one of the main factors in why restaurants become popular, and Jenny, who is a very good judge of food, says the restaurant's food is very good. So, there certainly might be some legitimate reasons to *consider* the idea of buying the restaurant.

However, there are many other factors to consider before making such a decision that your friend hasn't even mentioned. Why is it for sale? What do you and your friend know about running a restaurant? How much is the asking price? Even if you were to decide that buying the restaurant is a good idea, do you really want to be in a business partnership? If so, would your friend make a good business partner? These are just a few of the dozens of questions you would need to answer before agreeing to buy the restaurant with your friend. So, while there might be a good idea at its root, the argument isn't reasonable, because your friend hasn't presented nearly enough evidence to support it.

Logical Reasoning Basic Concept #3: Causality

Examining causality, or what most of us refer to as cause and effect, should help you determine the relative strength or weakness of a particular argument. Given that it is possible that *A* caused *B*, you then have to determine whether it is likely that *A* caused *B* or if there are other causal agents that are more likely to have caused *B*.

For example:

The store that burned down didn't seem to be doing well. I'm sure the owner torched it for the insurance money.

Is this a reasonable conclusion as to what caused the fire that burned the store down? No, it really isn't. It is an awfully long logical leap to say that because a store that burned down didn't appear to be doing well the owner probably set fire to it. For one thing, how do we know what kind of financial condition the store was in? Let's say we arrived at the conclusion that the store was struggling because we rarely saw customers going in or out. Well, there could be a lot of reasons for that. Maybe the only time we passed the store was on our way to and from work every weekday, and the store's peak sales occurred at night and on the weekends. It's also quite possible that, like many brick and mortar businesses these days, the store made far more money from selling merchandise over the internet than it did from walk-in traffic, but still had enough local customers that it was profitable to keep the doors open.

It's also quite conceivable that the business was only somewhat profitable but, for whatever reason, the owner didn't need for the store to make a lot of money and was quite content with the income he was bringing in. There are a great number of reasons why our notion that the store was in bad financial shape might be mistaken. However, even if our opinion about the financial health of the store is actually correct, it's still extremely unreasonable to conclude from that fact that the owner burned the store down to collect the insurance money. Tens of thousands of businesses go under every year in America, but commercial arson is pretty rare.

Now, let's add some more information:

The store that burned down didn't seem to be doing well. I'm sure the owner torched it for the insurance money. After all, he did spend three years in prison during the late 90's for hiring a guy to burn down another store he owned.

Hmm....this information certainly makes our conclusion that the owner torched the place look a lot less unreasonable, as the store owner has a history involving commercial arson. However, while our conclusion is not nearly as reckless as it was before, it's still not entirely reasonable to definitively conclude that he burned the store down. Many, many people who have been paroled after a conviction for conspiring to commit commercial arson never do such a thing again.

Let's add some more details:

The store that burned down didn't seem to be doing well. I'm sure the owner torched it for the insurance money. After all, he did spend three years in prison during the late 90's for hiring a guy to burn down another store he owned. On top of that, he owes $300,000 in gambling debts to some pretty unsavory characters. Furthermore, several local ex-cons have told the police that the owner offered them money to burn the place down. He also took out commercial insurance policies with three different companies last month. And there's no getting around the fact that surveillance cameras from a nearby business show him carrying what looks like a can of gasoline behind the store just before the fire started.

These new details completely change things. Assuming that the information is all true, is it still possible that the owner had nothing to do with his store burning down? Well, it may be theoretically conceivable, but it's virtually impossible for a rational person to believe. Based on the new information, it's not only reasonable to believe that he torched the place, it would be unreasonable to doubt it. The more evidence we have that supports a conclusion that *A* caused *B*, the more reasonable that conclusion is. At first, we had very little evidence to support the idea that the store's owner burned it down. However, as we were presented with more evidence, the link between *A* and *B* became pretty much indisputable. Of course, the cause and effect relationships you'll encounter on the Logical Reasoning section will be somewhere between these two extremes, but you'll use the same kind of reasoning process to analyze them.

In many instances, the test preparers will link a certain progression of evidence with a conclusion the evidence doesn't entirely support. The information given may be factual and reasonable up to a point, yet somewhere in the argument the examiners have made a leap beyond the bridge they were building with the evidence—or have loaded that bridge with more weight than it can support.

Consider this argument, remembering that you are only meant to determine whether, in this instance, the argument supports the conclusion (regardless of your personal opinion about the topic):

In the United States, over six million middle and high school students read significantly below grade level. American fifteen year-olds rank twenty-eighth out of forty countries in mathematics and nineteenth in science. Clearly, Americans are not spending enough on public schooling for their children.

For a multitude of reasons, many people would take this argument at face value, accepting the underlying assumption that all systems work better when they are given more financial support. That would be unreasonable, however, because there is very little evidence provided to support the conclusion. How much are we spending per student currently? How does that compare to what higher-ranking nations are spending? How is that money apportioned within the system? If the amount of money being spent isn't the issue, what are other countries doing that we are not? Has our ranking ever been higher and, if so, what were we doing then that we are not currently? In short, is lack of funding ultimately the primary cause of our poor scoring? If you were told the United States is tied for first in terms of spending per student, would you begin looking for other causes? These are all questions which must be considered before deciding that America doesn't spend enough on public schooling, and there are many more.

In the end, there may or may not be a link between the money we're spending on education and the test scores our students are achieving. The point is that accepting the argument requires you to make a huge mental leap in order to justify a conclusion that is not fully supported with the supporting statements. Also note (once again) that the LSAT designers count on the fact that you'll have a certain amount of ingrained bias in favor of a widely-held point of view. They take advantage of this to try to keep you from noticing the logical relationships that have been left out. Many test takers unintentionally supply the missing logical connections as a result of personal bias and lazy reasoning, and thus answer the question incorrectly.

Logical Reasoning Basic Concept #4: Acknowledging the Unknown

In our everyday verbal exchanges with others, it's quite common to pretend to know more than we do. There are several reasons we do this, among them a desire to avoid admitting ignorance of the topic at hand. We're not comfortable admitting that we're unable to connect all the dots someone else is presenting as a complete picture. Sometimes we're afraid we may have missed something, particularly if everyone else is nodding along in agreement, and we feel like we're the only one who doesn't know what is going on. You're eating lunch with a group of friends in the dining hall when another friend walks up and says "Oh, man, have you heard Adele's new song? Isn't it her best one yet?" All your friends are chiming in about how much they love it, and you're nodding your head and making statements to the same effect, despite the fact that you had no idea Adele even had a new single out. For that matter, some of your friends are probably faking it, too. We all do this sort of thing, and we do it constantly.

Well, that skill may work in conversation, at least occasionally, but it will get you nowhere on the LSAT. In fact, part of what the Logical Reasoning section of the LSAT is testing for is the ability to recognize and acknowledge what you do not know—to be fully aware of missing links, disconnected information, and facts that are irrelevant to the key issues,

Take a look at the following example:

Maude hates the city. Last year she moved her family to Montana.

The connection of statements makes it easy to conclude that Maude's reason for moving to a wide-open state like Montana is her hatred of the city. But is that really correct? Do you have enough evidence to conclude that is the case?

Casually linking the ideas in conversation is fine, but it will get you in trouble on the LSAT. Consider instead the universe of facts you don't know in this scenario. Using the analogy of a circle, what we do know fits inside the circle. What we don't know is everything outside that curving line.

First, what we do know: Maude's strong dislike of the city, where she moved, that she has a family of some sort, and very general timing of the move.

What we don't know: that's a much, much longer list. Does she hate all cities or one particular city? Why does she despise them (or it)? Was her move to Montana related to this preference or to some other reason, such as a job change or an urgent family situation? Is she trying to put distance between herself and someone from a failed relationship? Is she happily married, but seeking lots of room for her seven children to run around? Did she feel an urge to hop from state to state alphabetically and she just finished Missouri? What is her family made up of (kids, husband, cats?) and does its relevance in this statement go beyond the incidental? Obviously, we could go on and on.

The point is that there are many, many unknowns between the two statements above. Although some assumptions may be fairly reasonable given the information, and others may be a complete reach, it is still important to comprehend that they are assumptions and are not, in fact, *known*.

Logical Reasoning Basic Concept #5: Spotting Incomplete Arguments

One aspect of LSAT problem solving that we run into over and over is an argument that is somehow incomplete. This can lead to leaps in logic and incorrect assumptions – filling in the blanks. To the test preparers, any specific subject knowledge you may have is substantially less important than the mental skills you will use to identify underlying assumptions and missing pieces. So they will often deliberately pair a statement with a conclusion that doesn't quite match the given evidence, just to see how you deal with it.

First, you should bring to bear skills noted in Basic Concept #4: be aware of what you don't know in a given scenario. Don't assume facts. But here we take that skill one step further. Not only should you recognize what information is missing, you should also be able to identify the underlying assumption attempting to link the two. The following statement is presented to illustrate the point:

Merla's fingernail was chipped, so she stopped at the library.

Huh? In this case, it's obvious that there are missing links between the initial statement and the accompanying conclusion. What do Merla's nails have to do with stopping at the library? If we were provided additional information, like that a nail-care seminar is taking place at the library, this might make more sense, but there is certainly no obvious link between the two thoughts. However, it is unlikely the LSAT will employ such an obviously unrelated pairing. Try a more subtle example, like the one shown below:

A well-educated citizenry is required to maintain a free society. Robert has perfect attendance at school, so he must be well educated.

As above, it's important to first realize what you do not know. It may be reasonable to assume or it may even be true that Robert is well educated. However, you can't deduce that with any certainty from the above information. We would additionally need to know what is meant by a good education, the steps involved in procuring one (presumably it requires more than merely showing up for school), and how Robert measures up against those standards.

One way the LSAT may test your skills in spotting incomplete arguments is by asking you to identify the assumption in the given passage. In this case, you'd be looking for an answer choice like this:

b. Consistent school attendance results in a good education.

Or you might be asked which statement would most weaken the assumption underlying the author's conclusion. In that case, the correct answer could be something like this:

d. Some of our nation's founders, who were very learned men, never formally attended school.

First, identify what is incomplete in the argument. Dealing with the rest of the problem is easy after that.

The Most Common Question Types

Author's Main Point or Purpose

You should expect to see some questions about the author's main point or purpose on the Logical Reasoning section of the LSAT, as they are quite common. (Sometimes you'll be asked about the main idea; this is the same thing as the main point.) They are also among the easiest questions to answer correctly. In part that's because the passages in Logical Reasoning are so short; there's really no way to express several important ideas in so few words. Some of them might be harder than others, but in general, they're usually the questions that test takers have the least amount of trouble with in this section. It's also because the question itself is so straightforward and easy to understand. Every argument you'll come across on the exam has essentially two parts – a conclusion, and one or more premises. Premises are what the author bases his conclusion on. They're the facts or opinions he marshals in support of his conclusion. The conclusion and the main point are always the same thing, so once you've found the author's conclusion you've found his main idea. His *main point* is what he's trying to say, while his *primary purpose* is what he hopes to accomplish by saying it.

Here's an argument that features a Main Point question.

Professional sports associations must make some major changes if they want to stay in business. Drug use, violent crime, and irresponsible behavior are rampant in the NFL, NBA, and MLB and have been for years. It used to be that when people would think of professional athletes, they thought of outstanding people like Willie Mays, Hank Aaron, Roberto Clemente, Oscar Robertson, and Walter Payton. Now they are more likely to think of Mark McGwire, Jose Canseco, Barry Bonds, O. J. Simpson, Ray Lewis, and Rae Carruth. If something isn't done to get people like this out of professional sports, many fans will stop buying tickets.

Which one of the following is the main point of the passage?

There are a lot of people of bad character in professional sports.
People expect professional athletes to be good role models for children.
Pro sports leagues must take drastic action against illegal and immoral conduct of athletes.
Steroid use continues to be out of control in professional sports.
Today's athletes don't possess the same moral caliber of past generations of athletes.

The author clearly believes, and provides some evidence to back up his belief, that *there are a lot of people of bad character in professional sports.* Is that his main point, though? Let's not decide just yet, and keep going.

Does the author say that *people expect professional athletes to be good role models for children*? No, he does not, although that is certainly a reasonable inference of something the author believes. Of course, the author's main point can sometimes be implied as opposed to clearly stated. However, although this does seem like something he would feel strongly about, it certainly isn't his main point.

How about *steroid use has been and continues to be out of control in professional sports* or *today's athletes don't possess the same moral caliber of past generations of athletes.* Clearly the author strongly believes the latter, and probably believes the former, but he doesn't mention steroids specifically; only drugs in general. At any rate, neither one is his main point.

His main point is *pro sports leagues must take drastic action against illegal and immoral conduct of athletes*. This is almost a simple restatement of the first sentence of the passage, but not quite. The first sentence says that professional sports groups need to make major changes if they want to stay in business, while the next section of the article is about illegal and immoral conduct by athletes. It's clear that the major changes he recommends revolve around the bad behavior of athletes. (By the way, on the Logical Reasoning section of the LSAT, the first sentence of the passage is often the author's conclusion, although by no means is this always the case.)

Inference

Inference questions are also common on the Logical Reasoning section of the LSAT. They are more nuanced than Main Point questions, as they require you to read between the lines or put 2 and 2 together. They might ask you to determine what the author would agree or disagree with, based on the passage, even though there are no direct statements in the stimulus either for or against the position in an answer choice. Or they might ask you what a reasonable reader could infer from the passage, or what the author implied in the passage. *Imply* and *infer*, of course, are flip sides of the same coin – an author implies something by suggesting it without saying it directly. A reader infers something by forming a conclusion about something the author has not actually stated, by making logical deductions from one or more things he *has* stated. These questions can be phrased in various ways:

The researchers would most likely concur with which one of the following?
The Senator would be least likely to agree with which one of the following?
The argument most strongly supports which one of the following?
Which one of the following can be properly inferred from the passage above?

Here is an argument followed by a typical Inference question:

When you get right down to it, there are only two basic approaches to playing no limit hold 'em poker tournaments – long ball and small ball. Long ball is based on playing very few hands, but making large bets to either drive out opponents when bluffing or to build a huge pot when holding a strong hand. Small ball players take the opposite approach – they get involved in lots of pots by making small bets before the flop, hoping to make a great hand and trap their opponents or to bluff them out of the pot with nothing. Both approaches have their advantages and disadvantages. Choosing which one to use comes down to personal preference.

The author would most likely agree that:

The World Series of Poker tournament has gotten too large and takes too long

All poker players need to be skilled at both approaches to the game

Long ball players tend to win more tournaments

Small ball play is better suited for introverts

Bluffing is an essential skill for poker tournament success

The first answer is obviously wrong because it's completely irrelevant – the author says nothing about the size or length of the World Series of Poker or any other poker tournaments, and there's nothing in the passage to justify this inference.

How about *all poker players need to be skilled at both approaches to the game*? No; nothing like this is either stated or implied, either.

Does the author believe that *long ball players tend to win more tournaments*? No; if he did believe that, why would he say that choosing a style depends on personal preferences? If the long ball approach led to more success in tournaments, surely he would believe that that should be a major factor in choosing a playing style, and would recommend that approach to the game.

Would the author likely agree that *small ball play is better suited for introverts*? So far, this is the only answer that merits any consideration at all. After all, the author does say that choice of playing styles comes down to personal preference. However, he says absolutely nothing to indicate that he believes that small ball is better suited for introverts. This answer would trip a lot of people up because introverts tend to be shy and quiet, and the long ball style is highly aggressive, so it's natural for our minds to think the long ball style would be a poor match for introverts. However, there's no necessary correlation between personality and playing style and since the author doesn't say that he sees any connection between the two, we can't conclude that he would agree with this statement.

By process of elimination, that leaves *bluffing is an essential skill for poker tournament success*, which is the correct answer. We know that this is the right answer because all the others are wrong, but we can also verify it using logical deduction. The author says that there are only two basic approaches to playing poker tournaments, and then he describes each one, and both include bluffing. In other words, there are no playing styles that don't include bluffing. This means that he would have to agree that bluffing is an essential skill for poker tournament success.

Underlying Assumption

Another common question you'll encounter on the Logical Reasoning exam will ask you to select the answer which contains an assumption the author is relying on to make his argument. It's important to note that an assumption is *not* one of the author's stated premises, or the reasons he gives in support of his conclusion. Assumptions will never actually appear in the passage. Think of them as the unwritten premises standing alongside or behind the author's stated premises, which are the reasons he gives in support of his conclusion.

For example, in the argument, the author may conclude *D*, based on *C* and *B*. However, *B* or *C* actually hinges on *A* being true, even though the author never mentions *A*. So *A* is an assumption the author is relying on in order to make his case. It's important to keep in mind that assumptions are always unstated, because on most of these kinds of questions at least one of the answer choices will be a slight rewording of one of the author's stated premises. It will be incorrect, because if the author is stating something he is not assuming it, by definition. Also, while you will only be asked to pick out one, there will always be many, many assumptions underlying an argument. Consider this argument:

O. J. Simpson is a murderer. Murderers don't deserve recognition and honor. Simpson should be removed from the NFL Hall of Fame.

What assumptions is the author relying on? Several, actually, but here are just a few:

Media accounts of Simpson's activities just prior to and immediately after the murders of his ex-wife and her companion can be trusted.
Simpson wasn't framed for murder by racists in the Los Angeles Police Department.
He wasn't framed for murder by a corrupt prosecuting attorney's office.
The 12 jurors who found him not guilty were either incompetent or dishonest.
He (the author) has the capacity, at least in this case, to determine that someone is guilty of murder even though a jury has acquitted him.
Simpson is still in the NFL Hall of Fame.
Being in the NFL Hall of Fame is an honor.

We could go on and on, but that's plenty. These are all assumptions the author is relying on to be true if his argument is to hold water, even if he isn't consciously aware of all of them. If any of the above assumptions are wrong, then his argument falls apart.

That will always be the case if you have chosen the correct answer on an Assumptions question – if the author's argument doesn't fall apart if the assumption *isn't* true, then the answer is incorrect.

Because any time an argument *relies* on an assumption, if the assumption is turned on its head, then the argument *must* fall apart.

Let's return to a previous argument:

Professional sports associations must make some major changes if they want to stay in business. Drug use, violent crime, and irresponsible behavior are rampant in the NFL, NBA, and MLB and have been for years. It used to be that when people would think of professional athletes, they thought of outstanding people like Willie Mays, Hank Aaron, Roberto Clemente, Oscar Robertson, and Walter Payton. These days people are more likely to think of Mark McGwire, Jose Canseco, Barry Bonds, O. J. Simpson, Ray Lewis, and Rae Carruth. If something isn't done to get people like this out of professional sports, many people will stop buying tickets.
Which one of the following is an assumption on which this argument relies?

A large number of professional athletes are criminals or drug users.
Sports commentators are getting increasingly fed up with bad behavior by pro athletes.
In the past, the media helped cover up the immoral behavior of famous athletes.
Many people who buy tickets for sporting events base their decision to do so in part on the good behavior of athletes.
No athletes who use steroids have legal prescriptions for them.

Let's examine each answer choice.

A large number of professional athletes are criminals or drug users. Is this an assumption the author relies on? No. How do we know he's not assuming this? Because he states it expressly in the argument when he says that drug use and violent crime are rampant in the three big professional sports. An assumption, by definition, cannot be something that is stated in the argument.

- 65 -

Is he assuming that *sports commentators are getting increasingly fed up with bad behavior by pro athletes*? Well, if he is, there's really nothing in the argument to indicate that he's doing so. He doesn't mention sports commentators, writers, or analysts, and there's nothing in the passage that implies sports writers in general are getting tired of immorality and criminality on the part of the athletes they cover. While it's certainly possible that the author is himself a professional sports commentator, even if he is, he doesn't claim to be speaking for sports commentators in general, and the passage gives us no basis for inferring that other commentators share his view. Also, when in doubt, you should always run the reversal test of an assumption. So, ask yourself this – if this statement is wrong, would the author's argument fall apart? In other words, if sports commentators *aren't* getting more and more fed up with immoral and criminal athletes, would it ruin his case? No, it would not, because his argument is about the leagues losing revenue due to fed up *fans,* not sports commentators. Reversing the assumption doesn't destroy the argument, so this cannot be the correct answer.

In the past, the media helped cover up the immoral behavior of famous athletes. Does the author assume this in making his argument? No, he does not. If anything, he takes the opposite view, because he seems to believe that athletes of yesteryear really were better behaved than today's athletes, not that they were just as immoral but the media covered it up.

Many people who buy tickets for sporting events base their decision to do so in part on the good behavior of athletes. Does the author's argument rely on this assumption? Well, this answer certainly looks promising. The author argues that the major sports leagues must take serious action concerning the rampant bad behavior among its athletes if they want to stay in business. He says that, unlike in the past, when people today think of athletes, they think of drug users and violent criminals, and then he asks how long they will continue to keep buying tickets to see such players. So, clearly, he must be assuming that a large number of fans will stop buying tickets if something isn't done to crack down on the athletes' bad behavior, because fans don't want to pay to see a bunch of drug abusers and criminals. In other words, many fans buy tickets based in part on the good behavior of athletes. Now, let's reverse the argument: *few people who buy tickets for sporting events base any part of their decision to do so on the good behavior of athletes.* Does this destroy the author's argument? Yes, it does – if few people make decisions about buying tickets based on the good behavior of the athletes, then the presence of a large number of athletes who don't practice good behavior won't necessarily lead to significantly lower ticket sales. So this must be the correct answer.

Just to be sure, though, let's look at the last choice. *No athletes who use steroids have legal prescriptions for them.* Does any part of the argument rely on this assumption? No. In fact, the author doesn't mention steroids at all, but only drugs in general. It's a reasonable assumption that he's referring, at least in part, to major steroid scandals of the past several years. However, most people upset about steroid use in sports find their use scandalous regardless of whether or not the athlete has a legal prescription for their use. Even if every infamous steroid user in professional sports had acquired the drugs legally, using them is still against the rules of their leagues, as they give athletes a powerful, unfair advantage over their teammates and competitors who don't use them. Thus, even if the author is objecting to steroid use, he hasn't said anything at all to indicate that he's against their use only if they're not legally prescribed. If we run the reversal test we come up with *all athletes who use steroids have legal prescriptions for them.* Does this destroy the argument? No, because the author is denouncing rampant drug use in general, not simply the use of steroids for which they don't have legal prescriptions. In addition, drug use is only one of three factors he mentions. His argument also involves violent crime and irresponsible behavior.

- 66 -

New Information Questions

Another very common question type on the Logical Reasoning test requires you to analyze or reconsider the argument in light of new information. (This is the exact opposite of Inference questions, which require the test taker to *analyze new information in light of the argument.*) There are a few different types of these new information questions on this section of the LSAT. The two most common are Strengthen questions, and Weaken questions. They come in two forms. The first form simply asks which answer choice supports or weakens the argument or conclusion. The second one, however, asks you to select the answer which *most* strengthens or weakens the argument. In other words, you will have two or three answers which support/weaken the argument in some way, and you will need to select the one that does so most powerfully.

This second kind of question is usually phrased along these lines:

Which one of the following, if true, most strengthens the argument?
Which one of the following, if true, offers the most support for the conclusion?
Which one of the following, if true, most weakens the argument?
Which one of the following, if true, most undermines the author's conclusion?
Each of the following, if true, offers support for the argument EXCEPT: (this is actually a Weaken question)

You will see these sorts of questions on arguments where the premises don't strongly support the conclusion. In other words, the evidence is somewhat lacking – the premises make a case for the conclusion, but not one that is airtight and wholly persuasive. You'll be faced with five answer choices which each contain new information; at least one of them will definitely make the argument stronger or weaker, as the case may be.

It's important to note, however, that exactly how much the correct answer strengthens or weakens the argument can vary considerably. With one question, the correct answer might slightly damage the persuasiveness of the argument, while, with another, the new information contained in the right answer would cause the argument to fall apart completely. So the force of the new information is not an issue, in and of itself. It's only important when you have a *most* question, and new information in one answer is contrasted with the new information in other answer choices. For example, if you're looking for the answer which most strengthens the argument, don't simply choose the first answer that strengthens the argument in some way. It could very well be wrong, as there may be another answer which lends even more strength to the argument. Never forget the *most* in a question.

Also keep in mind that the LSAT designers like to trip test takers up on these kinds of questions by inserting answer choices containing information that seems powerful and relevant, but in reality has nothing to do with the author's actual conclusion, meaning it's actually completely irrelevant because it doesn't affect the argument at all.

Many people believe that advertising plays a major role in how people choose whom to vote for in presidential elections in America, but our recent study proves that this belief is a myth. We selected 5000 people, chosen from all 50 states in proportion to each state's percentage of the US population, and divided them into two groups. People in Group A each watched between 10 and 20 hours of television a week, while no one in Group B watched any television at all. Three months before the last election, we asked each person in both groups which presidential candidate they favored. Then, after the election was over, we asked each person whom they had voted for. At the beginning of the experiment, members of Group A favored the Republican candidate by a 51/49 margin, but wound up voting for him by a 56/44 margin. Group B favored the Republican candidate by a 52/48 margin at the start of the experiment, but voted for him by a 57/43 margin. So in both groups the percentage of actual votes for the Republican candidate was exactly five percentage points higher than the level of support at the beginning of the study, and the level of support for the Democratic candidate was exactly five points lower, proving that advertising does not make a big difference in presidential elections.

Which one of the following, if true, most weakens the argument?

The average number of years of college education in both groups was exactly the same.
The Democrats didn't spend quite as much as the Republicans on television ads.
Members of Group B spent an average of 15 hours a week listening to the radio.
Both candidates had high disapproval ratings.
Two television stations in Alaska refused to run any ads for political candidates.

Does the fact that *the average number of years of college education in both groups was exactly the same* weaken this argument? On the contrary, it would tend to strengthen it, since it reduces the likelihood that a difference in the demographics of the two groups influenced the results.

Let's look at three of the remaining answers together:
The Democrats didn't spend quite as much as the Republicans on television ads.
The Democratic candidate was tarnished by a late-breaking scandal.
Two television stations in Alaska refused to run any ads for political candidates.

Do any of these weaken the argument? Given the results of the study, it's not likely that the fact that *the Democrats didn't spend quite as much as the Republicans on television ads* was much of a factor, but theoretically it could have made a slight difference. If so, that would weaken the argument. Let's hang on to this answer.

Does the fact that *both candidates had high disapproval ratings* weaken the argument in any way? No, it doesn't. In fact, this answer is completely irrelevant. We can reject this answer choice out of hand.

Does the fact that *two television stations in Alaska refused to run any ads for political candidates* weaken the author's case for claiming that advertising doesn't play a major role when it comes to how people choose which presidential candidate to vote for? It's very unlikely, because the people in Group A were proportionally distributed across America. Alaska makes up a tiny percentage of the US population, meaning that very few (if any) members of Group A were affected by the lack of political ads on these two stations. So while it theoretically could have had a miniscule effect, it's very unlikely that it did, and even less likely that it had even the impact that lower spending on the part of the Democrats might have had. So we can discard this answer, too.

Let's examine the remaining answer choice. Would the fact that *members of Group B spent an average of 15 hours a week listening to the radio* weaken the argument? Yes, it would, since it would represent a huge blind spot in the study. The researchers appear to be assuming that the only way Americans can be exposed to ads for presidential candidates is by watching television. However, since the argument doesn't stipulate that fact, we have no reason to assume it's true while analyzing the author's case. Since it's common knowledge that radio stations run a lot of campaign ads during presidential campaigns, and there is nothing in the argument to the contrary, we can use this knowledge in our reasoning. When we do so, it's obvious that it would logically follow that people listening to the radio 15 hours each week would hear a large number of ads for presidential candidates. Since the author based the argument on the assumption that people in Group B weren't exposed to ads for presidential candidates, this information demolishes his case, making it the correct answer.

Most Strengthens Question

Public awareness campaigns have reduced the number of alcohol-related traffic fatalities in the US. One major factor in this reduction is the fact that many states now require persons convicted of driving under the influence of alcohol to install ignition interlock devices (breath analyzers) on their cars. These devices make it impossible for a car to be started when they detect alcohol on a person's breath. However, even after decades of efforts to reduce drunk driving, tens of thousands of Americans are still killed every year by drunk drivers, so more must be done. If Congress passed a law requiring car manufacturers to include ignition interlock devices on every new vehicle sold in America, eventually thousands more lives would be saved every year.

Which one of the following, if true, most strengthens the argument?

The number of alcohol-related traffic deaths dropped sharply in the late 1980s, but has since plateaued.
Rapidly improving technology is making it increasingly difficult for people to evade or defeat ignition interlock devices.
Because of the economies of scale, requiring ignition interlock devices on all vehicles would add less than $100 to the price of a new car.
Seven percent of alcohol-related traffic deaths are caused by people previously convicted of driving under the influence.
In a few years, iris recognition and vein matching technology will be incorporated into most ignition interlock devices, giving prosecutors extremely persuasive evidence in DUI cases.

The correct answer is D. Let's examine the answer choices in order:

The number of alcohol-related traffic deaths dropped sharply in the late 1980s, but has since plateaued. Does this strengthen the argument? No. The focus of the argument is the conclusion, which in this case is that a law requiring breath analyzers on all new cars would save thousands of lives every year. This statement *does* back up the sub-conclusion that more needs to be done about the number of traffic fatalities, but it provides no support for the idea that breath analyzers on every new car would save thousands of people's lives.

Rapidly improving technology is making it increasingly difficult for people to evade or defeat ignition interlock devices. Does this statement strengthen the argument? Yes, it does. If interlock devices are getting more and more effective, then that would make the impact of installing them on all new cars even stronger. However, the statement found in D does much more to strengthen the argument.

Because of the economies of scale, requiring ignition interlock devices on all vehicles would add less than $100 to the price of a new car. Although, if true, this statement would probably make the law more popular with the public and therefore easier to pass, it does nothing to strengthen the notion that installing breath analyzers on all new cars is an effective way to dramatically reduce the number of people killed by drunk drivers.

Seven percent of alcohol-related traffic deaths are caused by people previously convicted of driving under the influence. This is the statement that, by far, does the most to strengthen the author's conclusion. How so? Well, if seven percent of alcohol-related traffic deaths are caused by people who have already been found guilty of driving under the influence that means that 13 out of 14 deaths are caused by drivers who have *not* previously been convicted of DUI, and therefore don't have interlock device on their vehicles. Since we know from the argument that interlock devices have been a major factor in reducing the number of traffic deaths from DUI, and now we posit that at least 93% of the vehicles involved in DUI fatalities don't have one, it logically follows that installing them on all new vehicles would eventually dramatically reduce the number of drunk driving deaths in America.

In a few years, iris recognition and vein matching technology will be incorporated into most ignition interlock devices, giving prosecutors extremely persuasive evidence in DUI cases. Does this strengthen the argument in any way? No, it doesn't. The argument is about reducing the number of DUI fatalities, not about making it easier for prosecutors to convict people charged with driving under the influence. The statement neither strengthens nor weakens the argument; it is completely irrelevant.

Paradox Questions

For simplicity's sake, we've been referring to the stimuli on the Logical Reasoning exam as arguments, but not all of them actually are. Sometimes a stimulus will merely present a few facts without drawing a conclusion from those facts. If there's no conclusion in the text, there's technically no argument, and the stimulus is merely a reading passage. However, when referring to Logical Reasoning passages in general, it would be very awkward to keep saying "arguments and fact sets" repeatedly, so when we talk about Logical Reasoning arguments in general, we're referring to these passages, too.

Paradox questions take this form. Two or more facts are presented, and some of the facts will seem to be at odds with each other, and the question will ask you to resolve the problem by choosing the answer which resolves the paradox.

Paradox Question

> Medical researchers exploring the obesity epidemic in the US have made an intriguing discovery. With the cooperation of several restaurant owners, they observed and recorded thousands of diners eating lunch over the course of several months. As expected, they found that on average, seriously overweight people consumed far more calories while dining out than did people of average weight. However, when they compared calorie counts only among the seriously overweight diners, they were surprised to find that obese diners who were considered well-dressed consumed significantly fewer calories than did diners of the same weight who were considered casually dressed, even while eating at the same restaurant.
>
> Which of the following statements, if true, would provide the best explanation of the seeming paradox found by the researchers?
>
> Well-dressed diners tend to be more affluent and can more easily afford higher quality, less fattening food.
>
> In all weight categories, casually dressed people tend to eat more food when dining out than well-dressed people.
>
> Casually dressed diners tend to be less educated and therefore less informed about what constitutes healthy eating.
>
> Well-dressed diners tend to be more image conscious, so they eat less in public, but make up for it by eating more at home.
>
> The researchers had unconscious prejudices against people who are overweight and this affected their findings.

Before we examine the answer choices, let's consider the passage. Obesity researchers who studied thousands of lunch-time restaurant patrons over a period of several months discovered what seems to be a paradox. What is the intriguing finding? It's the fact that, on average, well-dressed obese people ate fewer calories than casually dressed obese people who weighed about the same.

What makes this a paradox? It's a (seeming) paradox because one would reasonably assume that in a study involving thousands of people, on average, people who weigh a certain amount would consume about the same number of calories as other people of the same weight. Yet, among obese people of approximately the same weight, there was a significant difference in the caloric intakes of well-dressed people and casually dressed people. Something doesn't add up here. How can casually dressed obese diners take in significantly more calories than well-dressed obese diners while weighing the same? It's your task to decide which one of the answer choices resolves the problem. Let's look at each one.

Well-dressed diners tend to be more affluent and can more easily afford higher quality, less fattening food. As a stand-alone statement, this makes perfect sense. It's common knowledge that when it comes to food, the lower the price, the more unhealthy and fattening the food tends to be. Keep in mind, however, that we're not concerned with whether the statement in any of these answer choices makes sense or not, because for the purposes of answering the question, we have to accept it as true.

So, assuming the truth of this statement, does it do anything to resolve the paradox? No, it does not. If well-dressed obese people are eating few calories because they have the means to afford less fattening food, then why do they weigh as much as casually dressed obese people who don't have that option? So the paradox still stands, and this answer is incorrect.

How about the next answer choice? *In all weight categories, casually dressed people tend to eat more food when dining out than well-dressed people.* Is this the answer we're looking for? No. It simply takes one part of the paradox – casually dressed obese people eat more calories when dining out than well-dressed obese people do – and applies it to everyone in general, irrespective of weight. While this explains that casually dressed obese people eating more calories when dining out than well-dressed obese people do is simply part of a larger pattern that holds true across the board, it does nothing to explain why two groups of obese people with different eating patterns weigh about the same.

Casually dressed diners tend to be less educated and therefore less informed about what constitutes healthy eating. This has a lot in common with A, and it's just as unsatisfactory when it comes to resolving the paradox. Instead of implying that casually dressed people eat poorly because they can't afford to eat healthy food, this answer states that they eat poorly because they're not educated enough to understand the principles of healthy nutrition. While this may very well be true, it does absolutely nothing to resolve the paradox. Because if well-dressed people make healthier food choices because they're better educated, why are they just as heavy as their less educated counterparts?

Well-dressed diners tend to be more image conscious, so they eat less in public, but make up for it by eating more at home. Right off the bat this looks more promising than the first three choices. Why? Because it includes a factor outside of the environment the researchers observed the diners in. That's in its favor, because logically there are very few factors within that environment which could explain how two groups of people can weigh the same despite significantly different calorie consumption patterns. However, that doesn't necessarily make this the correct answer. We have to decide if it resolves the paradox. Yes, it does, and it does so very well. The well-dressed obese diners eat less than their casually dressed counterparts in restaurants because they're self-conscious about their image, but at home, when no one's watching, they eat enough to make up for the caloric gap between themselves and the other group. This explains the paradox of why both groups weigh the same quite nicely. It's the correct answer.

The researchers had unconscious prejudices against people who are overweight and this affected their findings. This answer not only doesn't explain the paradox, it doesn't even make sense. However, since we're required to grant the truth of the statement in order to see if it's correct, let's think about it. Since the paradox involves two groups of overweight people, if the researchers had been biased against the overweight, whether consciously or unconsciously, they would have been equally biased against *both* groups, which, in effect, would mean that they would be treating both groups pretty much the same way. So this statement does nothing to explain why they found a discrepancy between the groups. Had the researchers been biased against well-dressed people or casually dressed people, that fact certainly could have played a role in the findings, but the notion that they were biased against the overweight explains nothing.

Keep in mind that the correct answer only needs to be the best explanation of the paradox out of the five choices given. It doesn't have to be the best explanation that's theoretically possible. For example, it's certainly possible that the average well-dressed obese person engages in more exercise than their casually dressed counterpart. This could explain the paradox, and might even do so better than D above. However, it's not one of the choices. Of the five answer choices we're given, D offers the best explanation of the paradox.

Flawed Reasoning Questions

With most of the questions you'll run into on the Logical Reasoning section of the LSAT, the reasoning in the stimulus will be basically sound. The author won't make any logical errors, and the premises will lead directly to the conclusion. Everything will work nicely together to form a solid argument. However, that won't be the case with every stimulus. In some cases, the reasoning found in the stimulus will be illogical in some way, and your job will be to figure out exactly what's wrong with the author's argument. These are Flawed Reasoning questions.

Sometimes the flaw will be fairly easy to spot, but in a lot of cases it will be much more subtle. In fact, many times it will be so subtle that if it weren't for the question asking you to name the flaw, many people taking the LSAT would never realize that the reasoning was illogical.

(This is one of the main reasons some people recommend reading the question before reading the stimulus, by the way. They say that if you know there's a reasoning flaw in the stimulus before you start reading it you can look for it as you read. They're right about that, but for other types of questions it's better to read the stimulus first, and because the vast majority of questions on the Logical Reasoning section aren't Flawed Reasoning questions, you'll come out way ahead if you read the stimulus first).

There are many different kinds of logical errors an author can make, but they all basically boil down to relying on a false or unjustified assumption: reasoning from only one case to a large number of cases, confusing correlation with causation, assuming that current conditions will continue unchanged, imprecision in numbers or measurement, making poor analogies, etc.

You'll be presented with five answer choices, only one of which will be the actual reasoning flaw in the argument. You must always keep in mind that it's likely that one or more of the answer choices will be red herrings – one of those wrong answers that have been carefully and deliberately designed to trap you into selecting it as your answer. On Flawed Reasoning questions, LSAT designers often trip people up by offering one or two answer choices which mention something the author actually does in the argument, but isn't illogical – it's actually valid reasoning.

Another common technique is to have one or more answer choices which refer to an error of logic which is common and well known, but isn't part of the author's argument. For example, an answer might say the author appeals to authority or the author assumed what he set out to prove, when the author has done no such thing. This second technique isn't as tricky as the first one, but you should definitely be on guard against it, too.

Here is an example of a Flawed Reasoning question:

It has been clearly demonstrated that the average married man earns more income than the average single man. Over two hundred scientifically rigorous studies have been done on this subject, starting nearly fifty years ago and continuing today, by such highly respected institutions as Harvard University, Yale University, and the University of Chicago. All told, these studies have included millions of men, from every level of education, all over the country, in hundreds of different occupations, and every one of them found that the average married man is paid more than the average single man. Obviously, there is widespread blatant discrimination in the employment market against men who aren't married.

Which one of the following best describes the flaw in the reasoning in this passage?

The author appeals to authority to make his case.
The author assumes what he is supposed to be proving.
The author fails to consider other possible causes than discrimination.
The author relies on insufficient or irrelevant data to make his case.
The author fails to use exact figures with respect to average incomes.

Let's look at the argument and consider the answers.

The author points us to over two hundred studies by highly respected organizations that compare the incomes of married men to the incomes of single men, which all found that married men are paid more than single men. He points out that this applies across the board, for pretty much all jobs and education levels, all over the country, and has been going on for a long time. He draws the conclusion that single men are being discriminated against by employers. We know from the question that there is a flaw in his reasoning. We have to determine what the flaw is.

Is it that *the author appeals to authority to make his case*? This sounds promising. A well-known logical fallacy is the appeal to authority and the author relies on studies for his evidence, and points out that some of them have been conducted by elite universities. So he's definitely guilty of committing the appeal to authority logical fallacy, right? Well, not so fast. While this would trip up a substantial number of test takers, it is not the correct answer.

While the author does cite some authorities, he is not committing the appeal to authority fallacy. Some people who have heard that appealing to authority is a logical fallacy seem to think that one can never cite an authority to back up an argument. This is nonsense; these people don't understand the appeal to authority fallacy. Appealing to an authority is only a logical fallacy if the authority has no expertise in the topic under discussion, or in a case where many other equally knowledgeable authorities disagree on the matter.

For example, if we're having an argument over Roman Catholic theology, and you quote a well-known Catholic theologian to back up your point, that is not a logical fallacy, because a Catholic theologian should certainly understand Catholic theology. However, if we're discussing which baseball player was the greatest ever and I say, "It's Babe Ruth because my priest said so," then I've committed the appeal to authority fallacy. Only an appeal to authority outside the subject matter, or a quote from one authority on a topic that is disputed among experts on the subject, are logical fallacies. Citing authorities who know what they're talking about is perfectly logical. So this answer is wrong.

Is *the author assuming what he is supposed to be proving*? This is another logical fallacy, known formally as begging the question. Here's a simple argument that begs the question: *Cigarettes are unhealthy because they're bad for you.* This argument begs the question because the conclusion is nothing but a restatement of the premise. Like a little boy who says his dad is always right, and his friend asks him how he knows, and the boy replies, "Because Dad said so," this is what's known as a circular argument. Does the author commit this logical fallacy? No, he does not. His premise, that married men make more money than single men, is not the same as his conclusion, which is that employer discrimination against single men is the cause of the disparity.

How about *the author fails to consider other possible causes than discrimination*? This one sounds like it might have some merit. Because it's the LSAT, we have to assume that the facts in the author's premise are correct, and that hundreds of studies have established that married men make more money than single men as an irrefutable fact. However, does it necessarily follow that discrimination against single men in the marketplace is the cause of this? Are there any other factors that could possibly be causing this phenomenon?

Couldn't experience be one factor that might be involved? Older men are more likely to be married than younger men, and older men are more likely to have more experience than younger men. Since employers usually prefer workers with more experience over those with less, it seems logical that they would pay them more. Another possible factor is motivation – doesn't it make sense that a man with a wife and/or kids might be motivated to work longer hours than a single man, and thereby earn more income? These are just two possible explanations of the pay disparity that don't involve discrimination, and the author didn't consider either one, let alone any others. So this is the correct answer.

What about *the author relies on insufficient or irrelevant data to make his case*? Why is this wrong? Well, if the author had mentioned only one study, he would not have much of a case. Instead, he pointed to over 200 studies by elite universities, involving millions of men from all walks of life, in hundreds of occupations, over a 50 year span, all of which came to the same conclusion. Assuming that the facts that the author cites in a stimulus are true, as we must do on the LSAT, it is clear that there is sufficient, relevant data to establish scientific consensus on this matter.

That *the author fails to use exact figures with respect to average incomes* is true, but completely irrelevant. The 200+ studies have established that there's a pay disparity between single and married men, and he is arguing that the mere existence of the disparity, not its size, is proof that there is widespread discrimination against single men in the workplace. Nothing in the argument requires exact figures to be stated.

Parallel Reasoning Questions

Parallel Reasoning questions are very common on the Logical Reasoning section of the LSAT, and you should expect to see a few of them when you take the exam. They can be more difficult to answer correctly than many of the other question types, so they typically eat up more of the clock you're racing against. That's because with Parallel Reasoning Questions, you're not just analyzing one argument; you're analyzing six – each of the answer choices is an argument, too. Because of this, we're going to spend more time discussing these questions than we spent on the other question types.

On Parallel Reasoning questions, the stimulus will be a very concise argument, comprised of only a few lines. After digesting the argument, you will then be asked to read the five answer choices, and select the one that contains the argument that most closely parallels the reasoning in the stimulus. LSAT designers have several ways of phrasing this, but they are all very similar, so there won't be any doubt that you're dealing with a Parallel Reasoning question. Analyzing and comparing five arguments to the original can take quite a bit of time, and this is another reason some LSAT guides recommend that you read the question before reading the stimulus. They suggest skipping all Parallel Reasoning questions, and only coming back to attempt them after answering all the other questions first.

It's your decision, of course, but we think you'll do better if you stick with our suggestion of reading the stimulus first. For one thing, you won't need to read the question in order to decide that you're looking at a Parallel Reasoning question. That will be obvious since the stimulus will be an argument that's only a sentence or two long. And, for that very reason, reading the stimulus first won't take much time at all, so how much time would you have saved anyway?

This is not to say that you should never skip a question and come back to it later. At times, that might be the wisest approach for you to take. It depends on how hard the question is. Some Parallel Reasoning questions are pretty tough to untangle, but, frankly, many are not that hard. If you get bogged down on one of these questions, by all means skip ahead and only come back to it if you've answered all the other questions. (You should always skip ahead if you get seriously stuck on *any* question on the LSAT, no matter what type of question it is.) It's inadvisable, however, to have a blanket policy that you're going to skip all Parallel Reasoning questions until the end, because of the fact that many of them are not particularly difficult. Since other kinds of questions can also be very hard, you could very well be skipping a question you could have easily answered only to run into another question that completely stumps you.

As the name implies, on Parallel Reasoning questions the correct answer must share the very same kind of reasoning found in the original argument. In other words, the two arguments must be similar in logical structure. If the original argument makes an analogy, then the correct answer will contain an analogy. If the stimulus relies on circular reasoning, the correct answer will, too. If the original argument reasons inductively, you'll be looking for an inductive argument in the answer choices.

In some cases the method of reasoning used in the argument won't be all that obvious or easy to discern, but that usually isn't a problem. The much bigger problem is that some of the answer choices will be so similar, or so opaque, that deciding which one best matches the reasoning in the original argument will seem to be a task whose difficulty falls somewhere between splitting hairs and reading goat entrails. To find the right answer, you'll need to consider and compare several aspects of the two arguments.

The first factor is validity. Sometimes the argument in the stimulus will be valid, in which case the correct answer must also contain a valid argument. Sometimes the stimulus argument will contain a logical flaw. In that case, the argument in the correct answer must also be invalid. You'll be able to know for sure if the argument in the stimulus is valid or invalid because if it's invalid, the question stem will say so. If the question stem doesn't use a word such as flawed, illogical, or questionable to describe the stimulus argument, then the argument is valid.

However, don't put too much weight on validity. It's definitely a requirement, but it's only one factor you must consider when looking for parallel reasoning. Or, to put it in formal logic terms - that the correct answer must match the validity or invalidity of the original argument is a necessary but not sufficient condition. Plus, it's very unlikely that only one answer choice will be valid or invalid, as the case may be.

Next you'll want to compare the conclusions in each argument. Remember, the stimulus and the five answer choices are all arguments, so they all *must* have conclusions (and at least one premise). The conclusion in the correct answer should have a lot in common with the conclusion in the original argument. This doesn't mean that the subject matter will be the same, or even similar. Nor does it mean that the two arguments must have the same placement of the conclusion with respect to the premises. The premises could come before the conclusion in the stimulus, and after the conclusion in the answer (or vice versa), and they could still be a match.

Two of the kinds of similarities you're looking for in conclusions are scope and certainty. These are functions of the language used in the arguments. When the conclusion in the stimulus contains broad, all-encompassing absolutes such as all, always, must, cannot, never, etc., then the conclusion in the correct answer must have the same scope, even if it's not expressed exactly the same way. For example, compare these two conclusions:

People over the age of 50 never win a marathon.
No person over the age of 50 ever wins a marathon.

These are both saying the exact same thing, even though only the first one uses the word *never,* and one sentence refers to *people*, while the other one uses *person*. So these conclusions are a match.

Now consider these two conclusions:

People over the age of 50 never win a marathon.
People over the age of 50 hardly ever win a marathon.

Are these two conclusions saying the same thing? No, they are not. The first one is making an absolute, categorical statement that a person over the age of 50 winning a marathon never happens. The second one is saying that it's rare for anyone over 50 to win a marathon, but it does not say it never happens. These conclusions do not match up.

So scope, or extent, is a very important clue when determining the correct answer for Parallel Reasoning questions. Certainty is another factor to consider. Consider these two conclusions:

Eating too much might cause you to get diabetes.
Smoking cigarettes will stain your teeth.

In the first one, it is stated that *A* could possibly lead to *B*, while in the second it is asserted that *A* definitely results in *B*. One conclusion is certain, while the other is indefinite, so these conclusions are not a match. Of course, there is quite a bit of overlap between scope and certainty; the main thing to keep in mind is to be on the lookout for any kind of an absolute. If the conclusion in the stimulus has an absolute, then the correct answer must too. If the conclusion of the original argument has an indefinite modifier, then an answer that contains an absolute is wrong. Because conclusions must match in scope/certainty, it's often the case that the argument in the correct answer contains some identical words or phrases as the original. This isn't always the case, and it also shouldn't be treated as a smoking gun level of proof by itself, but it can certainly be an important clue.

So tackle these questions by first seeing if the method of reasoning jumps out at you. If so, then you should generally be able to select the correct answer with no further analysis. If that's not the case, then consider validity, and eliminate all answers that don't match the argument for validity. If you still aren't sure, compare the conclusions for scope and certainty. In most cases, if you need to compare the conclusions in order to determine the right answer, doing so should be enough to enable you to pick the winner. However, if you're still unsure, then compare the premises in the stimulus with the premises in the answer choices, using the same principles just described above. If you're still unsure of the correct answer after that, then it's probably time to move on to another question.

Here is a sample Parallel Reasoning question:

Great college professors love to read. Bob has over a thousand books on his e-reader, so he would make a great college professor.

The flawed reasoning in which one of the following arguments most closely parallels the flawed reasoning in the argument above?

People with analytical minds are good at chess. Everyone in the accounting department has an analytical mind. Zelda works in the accounting department, so she would make a good chess player.

All baseball players can learn to switch-hit if they practice long enough. Jose Ramirez was the American League MVP last year, so he would be able to master switch-hitting in only a couple of weeks.

Everyone who works for an airline loves traveling. Derek has been an airline reservations clerk for seven years, so Derek loves traveling.

When the sky is red in the morning, it usually rains by the end of the day. The sky is red this morning, so it will rain today.

The best restaurant managers like to cook. Zoe throws some terrific dinner parties, so she would be a very good restaurant manager.

Let's look at this in depth.

First, why is this argument flawed? It's illogical because it the fact that great college professors love reading doesn't mean we can say that all people who love reading make great college professors. In other words, loving to read is a necessary condition for being a great college professor, but it's not a sufficient condition.

Is *A* the correct answer? In other words, does it have the very same flawed reasoning as the argument in the stimulus?

People with analytical minds are good at chess. Everyone in the accounting department has an analytical mind. Zelda works in the accounting department, so she would make a good chess player.

Let's break it down. It boils down to *all members of A are B, and all members of C are members of A, and D is a member of C, therefore D is B.* Is this reasoning flawed? No, it's not; it's perfectly valid. There's an extra step in there that might conceivably throw some people off, but it's a perfectly logical argument. Therefore it cannot be correct, as the correct answer must contain flawed reasoning.

Moving on to *B*:

All baseball players can learn to switch-hit if they practice long enough. Jose Ramirez was the American League MVP last year, so he would be able to master switch-hitting in only a couple of weeks.

Is this argument valid or invalid? It's invalid – while the premise says that all baseball players can learn to switch hit, there's nothing that says that the better a player is the faster he'll learn, let alone puts a time limit on the learning curve. This argument takes the premise too far and comes to an unwarranted conclusion. However, that is not the same kind of illogical reasoning the stimulus contains, so this answer is incorrect.

How about *C*?

Everyone who works for an airline loves traveling. Derek has been an airline reservations clerk for seven years, so Derek loves traveling.

This is a valid argument: *All members of A are B. C is a member of A, therefore C is B.* The logic is fine, but we're looking for an illogical argument, so this answer is incorrect.

Next we have:

When the sky is red in the morning, it usually rains by the end of the day. The sky is red this morning, so it will rain today.

This is pretty obviously flawed – it turns a likely outcome (*usually rains*), into an absolute certainty (*will rain*), but it's not the kind of flawed reasoning we're looking for, so it's out.

By process of elimination we know that *E* must be correct, but let's look at it to find out why.

The best restaurant managers like to cook. Zoe throws some terrific dinner parties, so she would be a very good restaurant manager.

First, notice that the language and structure are very similar, but not identical. This is a good sign. More importantly, though, if we break the logic down we'll see that it has the very same flawed reasoning. Just because the best restaurant managers like to cook, it doesn't necessarily mean that people who like to cook would make great restaurant managers. Enjoying cooking is a necessary condition for being a great restaurant manager, but it's not a sufficient condition. This is the very same illogical reasoning found in the stimulus, so it's the correct answer.

Less Common Question Types

The majority of the questions you'll encounter on the Logical Reasoning section of the LSAT will fall into one of the question types we've just discussed. That's why we spent so much time dissecting these particular types of questions and explaining how to solve them. However, there are many other kinds of questions used far less frequently by the test designers. You won't see a question from each of these categories on the LSAT when you take it, but you'll definitely run into some of them. It's not necessary to spend nearly as much time prepping for these questions, but you should make sure you're familiar with them before taking the exam. So, here are some other Logical Reasoning question types you can expect to see when you take the LSAT.

Passage Completion Questions

On a Passage Completion question, the last part of the final sentence of the passage is left blank, and the question stem asks you to choose the answer which best completes the passage. On these, the correct answer should not only make logical sense; it must also fit with the rest of the passage structurally and stylistically. Because of this, it's usually not very difficult to select the right answer. At least two of the choices won't make much sense as an ending for the passage, and the other incorrect choice(s) won't be a good fit when it comes to structure or style.

Must Be True | Deduction Questions

While these are phrased differently, they are essentially asking the same thing as Inference questions. Just follow the principles for solving Inference questions when you run into a question asking you something like, "Based on the passage, which one of the following must be true?" or "Which one of the following statements can be deduced from the passage?"

Point at Issue Questions

Two brief, conflicting statements will be given, each from a different person, and the question stem will ask you to choose the answer which properly conveys the point at issue between the two. The key here is to ignore the noise in the arguments, such as extraneous details, and boil each statement down to its essence. When you do that, the dispute will become clear, and it will reveal the correct answer.

Conclusion Questions

Every now and then you'll see a question asking you to identify the author's conclusion. Don't let the wording on these questions fool you. Remember, the conclusion is the main point the author is making. In other words, these are simply Main Point questions. Follow the principles described in that section and you'll be fine. Always keep in mind that the test designers like to include a premise or two as answer choices, which trips many people up. Don't let that happen to you; make sure you don't choose an answer simply because it contains a reframing of a statement from the argument – the statement that is restated must be the conclusion.

Argument Proceeds By | Method of Reasoning Questions

These questions ask you to choose the answer which best describes the method of reasoning employed by the author, or best shows how the argument proceeds. In other words, the conclusion is not the focus, nor is any inference or deduction which can be made on the basis of the argument. The validity of the argument is also not a factor. The only thing that matters for these questions is how the author makes the argument. Once you identify how the argument is structured, the key to answering these questions correctly is to mentally eliminate the fluff in the answer choices and focus on essentials. Because there aren't very many ways of coming up with incorrect but credible answer choices which can deceive many test takers if written in straightforward language, the LSAT designers tend to employ verbosity and bombast as distractions. That is, they use too many words, or intellectual-sounding language, or both, to gussy up the answer choices to make the wrong answers sound more appealing. When you strip away all the fancy verbal footwork, you'll find that choosing the correct answer is often fairly easy.

Syllogism Questions

A syllogism is a classic argument structure used in formal logic. It contains two premises, and a conclusion. Here's a basic syllogism:

When the sun is up it is daytime.
The sun is up.
It is daytime.

You will likely encounter a question or two featuring syllogisms on the Logical Reasoning section of the LSAT. The stimulus will present a syllogism, and then ask which of the answer choices must be true if the syllogism is true. Syllogism questions are probably the most straightforward and easy to understand questions you'll come across in Logical Reasoning. For that reason, they are also some of the easiest to solve. You may find it helpful to draw a diagram illustrating the syllogism, but in most cases that won't be necessary.

Other Question Types

Every now and then the folks at LSAC come up with a new question type, so it's possible you may run into a kind of question that's never before been seen on the LSAT exam. Plus, we have omitted a few question types from this guide because they only rarely appear on the test, and many of them are very close to fitting into one of the categories we've discussed. So if you encounter a question that doesn't fit into one of the listed categories, there's no need to panic. Logic is logic; if you've used this guide to practice, and you've mastered the skills necessary to tackle the kinds of questions discussed at length in this book, you'll be ready for any curveball the LSAT designers throw your way.

The Writing Sample

How Important Is It?

Reading and writing are a daily part of life for law students and for lawyers. An ability to express your thoughts concisely, clearly, and persuasively in a number of styles from court briefs to personal letters is critical to doing well in the profession. This need for attorneys to possess a mastery of writing skills was ostensibly the primary reason for adding a timed writing section to the LSAT. Another reason often cited is that a writing sample gives the admissions committee a more well-rounded picture of a law school candidate, allowing them to make more holistic decisions about who gets in and who doesn't.

However, there are many people who believe that the Writing Sample is nothing more than window dressing; a sort of diversionary tactic. Law schools have been widely criticized in the past for focusing too much on numbers (i.e., test scores and grade point averages) in making admissions decisions. Critics asserted that this was unfair to many deserving candidates who are perfectly qualified to do well in law school but don't do well on standardized tests, and that law schools' narrow minded focus on test scores and GPAs resulted in an imbalanced pool of new lawyers which was stultifying the legal profession.

Law schools dug in their heels for years and resisted changing the test, but they eventually gave in. However, the Writing Sample is unscored and there is little evidence that it has much of an effect on admissions decisions. Some observers insist that it can have a small effect, but almost no one believes that the Writing Sample is really very important when it comes to getting into law school.

Nevertheless, many people who are preparing to take the LSAT have a lot of anxiety about the Writing Sample part of the exam. As you can see, this shouldn't be the case, because the answer to the question of how important the Writing Sample is when it comes to law school admissions falls somewhere between not very important and not important at all. If you've been stressed about the Writing Sample, this should help relieve your anxiety.

Another thing to keep in mind is that if you have what it takes to get good grades in college and a high score on the LSAT, then you almost certainly possess all the skills you need to do well on the Writing Sample. On the other hand, if you lack the skills necessary for success on the other sections of the LSAT, then it won't matter how well you do on the Writing Sample. Also, you will not be expected to produce the kind of writing that appears in magazines or wins literary prizes. Nor will you be trying to craft persuasive arguments for why you'd make a great law school student, as this is not an admissions essay.

You will be given 35 minutes to write a two page essay taking a position on a question and explaining the reasoning behind your argument. Your writing will demonstrate that you have the ability to think on your feet, look at problems from various angles, organize your thoughts, and express yourself clearly and concisely. These are all skills that will be vital to your success in law school and as a working attorney, and which you should be very good at by this stage in your academic career. So there is really no reason you should be filled with anxiety about the writing portion of the LSAT. However, you should be prepared to do your best on this part of the exam, if for no other reason than there is an off chance that your essay might be the tiebreaker in a close admissions decision.

Do not misunderstand – it is not acceptable to leave the Writing Sample blank, to turn in a humorous essay, or to put only a half-hearted effort into writing it. You also should not choose another topic to write about other than the assigned one. Law schools can and do reject applicants for this kind of behavior, and you should strive to do your very best on this section of the exam. We're simply saying that you should not stress yourself by worrying about the Writing Sample, because in the vast majority of cases it simply isn't a decisive factor in the admissions process. If you're prepared and give it your best on test day, you should do just fine. In this section, we'll you show what you need to know in order to be fully prepared for success on the Writing Sample.

The Writing Sample Format

The Writing Sample isn't the typical kind of essay most people have in mind when they think of an essay. Typically, an essay is fairly open ended. There is usually an assigned topic or subject, but the essay writer is allowed a lot of leeway when it comes to choosing how to address the topic. That is not the case with the Writing Sample on the LSAT. It has a very specific format, one which has been deliberately designed to test some of the most important skills a person will need to succeed in law school and a subsequent legal career.

You will be given a brief prompt to read. It will describe a choice that a person or organization is facing. Usually the choice will be along the lines of the following scenarios:
- Choosing one of two non-profit groups to support with corporate giving
- Selecting one of two new international markets to enter
- Selecting one of two new product lines to develop
- Choosing one of two candidates for promotion to regional vice-president
- Choosing one of two locations for the new company headquarters

You will be given a description of two criteria, such as needs or goals, which are important or desirable to the person or organization. These considerations will usually not be complementary; in fact, they will usually be very different, and may even be at odds with each other. Finally, you will be given descriptions of two people or things which are under consideration.

You will be given two sheets of paper, and you will have a 35 minute time limit. You will also have scratch paper to use in this portion of the LSAT. Your task in the Writing Sample will be to argue that one of the candidates or alternatives is a better choice than the other one. Always keep in mind that there is no right or wrong answer; it doesn't matter which choice you make. This aspect of the essay trips many people up, as they see it as yet another test of logic and reasoning. They believe that an important part of doing well is choosing the correct alternative, and that if they give it enough thought one candidate will clearly stand out as a better choice than the other one.

This is not true; in fact, it's the exact opposite of the truth. In the descriptions it will be clear that each option has both strong and weak points and that one will be better suited to meeting one of the two provided criteria, while the other will be a better match for the other criteria. The criteria and candidate descriptions are deliberately written in such a way that each alternative would be a good choice. Your job in the Writing Sample is simply to pick one of the alternatives and make the best case you can for it. Since both alternatives are fine, it's impossible to pick the wrong one.

Another thing to keep in mind is that you won't need any knowledge of the particular aspects of the factors the prompt asks you to consider. If the prompt is about which location an advertising firm should choose for its new offices, for example, you won't be expected to know anything about advertising or commercial real estate in order to write your sample. All the information you need will be provided in the prompt, and you should not spend any of your very limited time thinking about these irrelevant factors.

You should have several goals for your essay:

- It should be completely focused on the prompt. You may include ideas or facts that aren't mentioned in the prompt as long as they have a bearing on the decision making process. Any information that isn't germane to the decision should be left out.
- It should come across as an organic whole. In other words, even though it is only two pages long, the separate components should work together so that the essay strikes the reader as a well-organized and consistent piece of writing that flows logically. It should have a distinct opening, a main body, and a clear conclusion.
- It must be a strong argument, backed up with facts and sound reasoning. You want to state your case persuasively, and to do so you need to bolster your decision by demonstrating exactly and specifically how your choice is the better one, based on the candidate descriptions and the criteria supplied in the prompt.
- It should incorporate the characteristics of good writing. As we pointed out earlier, your essay doesn't need to be a masterpiece, but it should be well written. That means it should hold the reader's interest. You should use proper grammar and spelling, of course. You should also try to demonstrate a great command of vocabulary, while making sure not to misuse any words in an effort to impress. It's also important to use a variety of sentence structures. An essay with mostly long sentences is boring and hard to follow, while one with mostly short sentences is jarring and unpleasant. You need to write as legibly as possible. If necessary, use block print instead of cursive.

Writing Sample: Your Action Plan

Planning

Carpenters have a saying that can help you craft a great Writing Sample – measure twice, cut once. The meaning is that measuring only once often leads to having to make two cuts, wasting time and possibly material. In other words, it's better to play it safe by measuring twice, even though doing so takes longer than doing the bare minimum. This adage is a pithy expression of the critical importance of taking enough time to properly prepare for a task. Of course, unlike carpenters who can start over with another piece of wood if they make a mistake, you won't get a second chance, so it's even more imperative to take some time to plan your essay before you start writing it.

Start by reading the prompt all the way through, taking your time and not rushing. Then do it again. Use the scratch paper provided to make a note of things that will be important for you to incorporate into the essay. You should really concentrate on the candidate descriptions, and the criteria given to guide you in your choice, as these will be the key points you need to cover in your essay.

While it's important not to rush the planning of your essay, you should decide as quickly as possible if you're going to argue for choice A or choice B. It may be that you're able to decide which choice to support immediately after your first reading of the prompt. If that turns out to be the case for you, you're off to a great start. If you're still having trouble making a choice even after your second reading, there's no need to panic, because there is an easy way to make your decision, which we'll get to in a moment.

Whether or not you've made a clear choice as to which option to argue for, it's time to make a couple lists. On your scratch paper, make a separate heading for each choice. Under each heading, quickly list all the pro and cons you can think of with regard to that option, based on the criteria in the prompt. Don't spend too much time thinking about this step. It isn't complicated; most of the pros and cons should be pretty clear from your reading of the prompt. If you've already made your choice, once you have your lists of pros and cons for each candidate, you can begin the writing process. If you haven't yet been able to make your decision, now is the time to choose *A* or *B*.

How? It's very simple - when you have finished making both lists, one is likely to have more pros than cons. If so, make that the one you argue in favor of. If both options are close to being equal, just flip a coin and pick one and stick with it. The point is to write about the one you think it would be easier to make a case for. If they're relatively equal, then that becomes a moot point, because you should be able to make a good case for either of them. We can't stress enough that there is no right answer, and it's important to keep that in mind. It will be very easy to get distracted and make the all too common mistake of trying to decide which choice is better. Don't let it happen to you – either choice is fine. It's how you make your case that counts.

Ideally you should spend no more than about 5 minutes on planning your essay.

Writing

Once you have made your lists of the pros and cons for each alternative, and you've chosen which one to argue for, it will be time to begin writing. The clock will be ticking, and you will need to create two pages worth of solid reasoning and writing in a very short time. This will be a real challenge, but there's no reason you can't accomplish it, especially if you've built a solid foundation by going through the planning steps outlined above. Depending on your handwriting, it will take between 400 and 600 words to fill two pages. This is not a lot of words; it adds up to four to six short paragraphs. The challenge for most people will be the quality of their writing, not the quantity.

Some Common Mistakes to Avoid

Don't use an artificially large script in an effort to fill the pages more easily. It will be obvious that you did so, and such a blatant attempt to game the Writing Sample will leave a very negative impression on any readers.

While writing your essay, you should assume that you're writing for a person who is familiar with the prompt you're writing about. There's no need to begin by rehashing the scenario, or outlining the main facts or questions. Doing so would not only be redundant, but might also be viewed as attempting to pad your essay with non-essential material. There's absolutely no need to restate the problem, and doing so can only weaken your Writing Sample. (Of course, when you're giving your reasons for preferring *A* or *B*, feel free to refer back to the decision criteria and the candidate descriptions in order to demonstrate why your choice is the better option. That isn't padding your essay with fluff; it's giving proof to back up your argument.)

Another thing to avoid is the generic open, which is a commonly used method of padding a written piece. Don't begin your essay by stating obvious facts which have only a tenuous connection to the prompt and do nothing to advance your argument.

Here are some examples of a generic open:
- "In today's economy, it's critical that companies promote the best candidate...etc."
- "Taking care of the elderly is expensive, and the aging of the Baby Boomers means...etc."
- "Choosing which college to attend is one of the most important decisions a person...etc."

Along these same lines, do not write about how difficult it is to make the decision because each alternative would make a good choice, and both have strengths and weaknesses, etc. As the prompts are written precisely to create a situation in which a person or organization is faced with a difficult decision, this would only be stating an obvious fact which does nothing to help persuade the reader that your choice is the correct one.

Do not be informal. The tone of your writing should be semi-formal. It does not need to be as formal as a doctoral dissertation, but neither should it read like something you wrote to a friend. Also, write your essay in the third person. *I* and *you* are two words that should never appear in an LSAT Writing Sample.

Do not use superlatives such as best or most qualified when comparing the two alternatives to each other. Superlatives should only be used when discussing three or more people or things. Use the comparative forms such as better or more qualified when comparing the choices in your Writing Sample, because only two are involved.

The Opening

For many people taking the LSAT, coming up with the opening is the most difficult part of writing a good essay. It's easy to waste a lot of time trying to think of a good opening and time is precious on the LSAT. Each minute you spend thinking about this is one less minute you will have for the actual writing, so you need to be ready to put pencil to paper as soon as you've finished your planning.

The format of the prompt makes this easy to do, fortunately. Your essay should essentially be a piece that simply compares and contrasts the two possible choices in light of the criteria in the prompt. Because you are so constrained in the way you should handle the subject matter, there is much less room for error when it comes to stylistic choices. There is no need to attempt to be creative or open with some elegant rhetoric. Instead, you should simply get right to the point and state that *A* or *B* is the better choice.

At first glance this suggestion that there is one ideal way to begin your Writing Sample may sound limiting. It *is* limiting; deliberately so. However, limitations are not always negative and they can prevent a lot of bad things from happening. Many of the law school hopefuls sitting for the LSAT will turn in a poor Writing Sample because they spent far too much time trying to decide how to get started. Indecision is a luxury a person cannot afford on the LSAT. That's why deciding right now that you're going to begin your Writing Sample by declaring which option is better is the best way to go. The fact that it's also the opening style that is best suited to the format of the Writing Sample makes the decision even easier.

There are several effective ways of phrasing your opening, but it will always be some version of *"A is the better choice, and here is the broad reason why"*. (The body of your essay will flesh out the why.) Here are a couple of examples:

- Acme should choose Jenkins for the promotion, because his years of experience in the field will be more valuable to the company than Smith's advanced degree.
- Smith's possession of a Ph.D will give Acme much needed credibility in the market, and this makes him the superior choice to Jenkins.

The Body: Contrasting the Choices

(For the rest of this section, A will denote the option you chose to argue in favor of, and B will denote the one you rejected.)

After a brief opening in which you declare that *A* is better, you will move into the heart of your essay, which will consist of arguments as to why that is the case. In other words, you'll be backing up the claim you made in your opening with actual evidence. You will do this by contrasting *A* with *B*, demonstrating how *A*'s strengths outweigh *B*'s strengths, and showing how *B*'s weaknesses outweigh *A*'s weaknesses. This will be somewhat subjective, of course, because the two choices will usually be pretty evenly matched, as we pointed out earlier.

You should not worry about that. The fact that either choice would be fine is immaterial; the only thing that matters is your ability to write and reason well on the topic. The scenarios are created in such a way that you should easily be able to think of a few areas in which *A* is stronger than *B*, and vice versa. You should be careful to avoid the glaring mistake of discussing only the strengths of *A* and the weaknesses of *B*. An essay that mentions only those factors in *A*'s favor will come across as having been written with blinders on. Your Writing Sample should strike the reader as balanced and evenhanded, not as lopsided and tendentious.

You will have more leeway in writing the body of your essay than you did in writing the opening. There are several ways you can effectively structure your argument in favor of *A*, and none of them is necessarily better than the others. No matter which structure you choose, you will be ready to start writing immediately because you made a list of the pros and cons for each candidate in your planning stage. Now you will take them and expand on them. You may introduce elements that aren't mentioned in the prompt, as long as they are common knowledge. You could use the fact that gas prices are of growing concern, for example, if that were germane. However, extraneous information should always take a back seat to the given criteria.

One good way to write the body is to start with the decision making criteria given, and examine each candidate in light of them. For example, assume that you're being asked to choose which new product a company should introduce, and the two criteria given are to 1) gain market share, and 2) raise profit margins. In this approach, you would examine both choice *A* and choice *B* for effectiveness in meeting the first goal. Then you would compare and contrast them in light of the second goal.

Another good approach is to thoroughly cover all the strengths and weaknesses of *B*, followed by an examination of the strengths and weaknesses of *A*. If you decide to use this structure, it's best to start with the choice you're rejecting and end with your preferred choice, as this makes for a stronger essay.

A third variation is to begin by comparing the weaknesses of *A* and *B*, and then going on to compare their strengths. You should end with the strengths for the same reason you should end with your choice of candidates in the previous structure – it makes for a stronger essay.

Any of these structures will work well. There are other ways of organizing your argument, but you should choose between one of these three, as other approaches tend to come off as disorganized and ineffectual. Finally, you should decide which writing structure you are going to use before test day. It will be one less thing you have to think about during the LSAT. You cannot afford to waste any time trying to decide how to format your argument, so make sure you know which one you will use before you walk into the testing center, and stick with it.

The Conclusion

Your writing sample will only be 400 – 600 words long, which doesn't leave a lot to work with when it comes to writing a conclusion. This is not really much of a problem, though, because the format of the Writing Sample doesn't require a strong conclusion. Unlike a thesis or a research paper, the Writing Sample is essentially nothing but one long conclusion. You begin by saying *"A is the best choice, and here is the broad reason why."* You then go on to flesh out the why in the body of your essay. After that, having a powerful conclusion set off from the rest of the essay would be difficult to pull off. Even if you could make it work, it would be redundant.   All you really need is an effective way to end the essay. Something along the lines of *"These are the reasons Jenkins is the superior choice"* will be just fine. The last thing you want to do is simply repeat what you've just said in the body of your essay.

Your Writing Sample should consist of four to six paragraphs, and you should spend no more than 25 minutes writing it.

Reviewing and Editing

Once you've finished writing your essay, you should have at least five minutes left. You should use that time to proofread it and correct any errors that you find. Misspelled words are common, but they are hardly the only thing to be concerned about. Other errors to look for are vague or mismatched pronouns, dangling modifiers, lack of subject/verb agreement, wrong verb tense, etc. Do your best to find and correct all errors, while keeping an eye on the clock. You do not want to be in the middle of making a correction when the time limit is reached.

Example Prompt and Writing Sample

Acme Kitchen Appliances is entering the Latin American market and is trying to choose which candidate to hire to lead the effort. Write a brief essay making your best case for choosing one or the other candidate. Keep these two criteria in mind when making your choice and writing your essay:

1) The company wants to establish a reputation as a provider of kitchen appliances of the highest quality that are worth paying more for.

2) Acme seeks to establish a presence in each Latin American country as soon as possible in order to build cash flow and make the division self-sustaining.

Raul Gonzales heads up the Latin American sales department for a top US-based soft drink company. Before that, he was a regional vice-president for one of Mexico's largest snack companies. Gonzales has 25 years of business experience in Latin America, and he has traveled extensively in the region.

James Anderson is the vice-president for marketing for the US division of a large Asian automobile manufacturer. In his 20 year career at the firm, the company has gone from being perceived as a maker of low priced cars of shoddy quality to a company that makes stodgy but reliable mid-priced cars.

Acme Kitchen Appliances should choose Raul Gonzales to lead their entry into the Latin American market, as he is a better choice than James Anderson. His 25 years of experience all over Latin America will be an important asset as the company seeks to build its business south of the border.

At first glance, Anderson might seem to be the better choice in light of Acme's goal of establishing a reputation as a provider of expensive but high quality kitchen appliances. Upon further analysis, however, that first impression does not hold up. While it's true that Anderson has helped improve the image of his company over the past two decades, the automaker's products are seen as dependable but dull, and they don't command premium prices.

Anderson's achievement is impressive, but there is no indication that he has what it takes to persuade Latin American consumers that Acme's kitchen appliances are the highest quality products available and they should pay a lot of money for them. Furthermore, this kind of brand imaging can take years, if not decades, to create in the minds of the public.

Acme's second consideration of establishing a market in every country in the region should take priority in choosing whom to hire, as this is likely to be much more easily achieved than creating a brand identity as a high end product right out of the gate. Once they have a foothold and a self-sustaining Latin American base, they can then work on creating an image of a top of the line manufacturer.

This is why Raul Gonzales is a much better candidate for the position than James Anderson. While it's true that his marketing experience has been with companies selling low priced food and drinks, he has decades of extensive experience in the entire region. He has thousands of business contacts, in every Latin American country; James Anderson has spent his entire career in the US. Gonzales grew up speaking Spanish; Anderson would need a full time interpreter if he took the job.

Gonzales doesn't just have the contacts and the language skills necessary for the task; he also has 25 years' worth of intimate knowledge of the culture and business practices of the Latin American market. His career success is a clear indicator that Gonzales is a man who can open doors and sell products in Latin America. Establishing a foothold in the market should be Acme's first priority, and in that regard, James Anderson simply can't compete with Raul Gonzalez, who is clearly the better candidate for this position.

Practice Test

Section I

<u>Directions:</u> The questions in this section are based on the reasoning given in brief statements or passages. It is possible that for some questions there is more than one answer. However, you are to choose the <u>best</u> answer; that is, the response that most accurately and completely answers the question. You should not make assumptions that are by commonsense standards implausible, superfluous, or incompatible with the passage. After you have chosen the best answer, blacken the corresponding space on your answer sheet.

1.   The vast majority of extant music from the medieval period is recorded on manuscripts. The production of medieval manuscripts was very costly, because all manuscripts were painstakingly copied by hand onto an expensive form of parchment. As a result, few people   were able to produce or own them, and the Catholic Church, which had literate scribes as well as considerable wealth, produced and maintained most manuscripts during the Middle   Ages. Any medieval music not recorded on manuscripts has now been lost to history. Most of the medieval music still in existence is sacred music.

The claims made in the above passage, if true, best support which of the following statements?

(A)   The greatest music of the medieval period was sacred music, and for this reason it was recorded on manuscripts.

(B)   Because the Church did not value popular music, the scribes were not allowed to copy it onto manuscripts.

(C)   As the Catholic Church was the center of medieval life, popular music paralleled sacred music very closely.

(D)   In addition to the Church, many wealthy aristocratic households held large numbers of music manuscripts.

(E)   Because the Church primarily recorded sacred music on manuscripts, historians are unable to confidently describe medieval popular music.

2. The CEO of a major fast-food chain just released a statement indicating that the chain has revamped its ingredient list and revised its menu options so that all selections on the menu are now healthier than any of the menus from competing fast-food chains. Among the changes that will be made, the fast-food chain will be eliminating unsaturated fats and downsizing portions. He claims, "We've heard the request of our customers for healthier meals, and with the changes we're making we'll be offering our customers better choices. Our customers will now have healthy fast-food options that put all other fast-food chains to shame."

Which of the following, if true, most seriously undermines the CEO's claim of offering healthier selections to customers?

(A) While the fast-food chain is improving certain ingredients, they are still including additives that tend to make customers addicted to the fast food.
(B) The CEO is receiving a large bonus for the potential boost in sales that the new menu options are expected to bring.
(C) A focus group unanimously complained that the food was bland and not as tasty as items on the previous menu.
(D) The fast-food chain has begun marketing heavily to children, encouraging children to ask for the healthier options when ordering in a restaurant.
(E) The fast-food chain has not removed many of its previous menu items but has instead simply replaced the unhealthy ingredients with healthier options and reduced the portion sizes.

3. The largest public health organization in the country has raised concerns about the herbal sweetener stevia, claiming that it has conducted extensive testing and that in its opinion the dangers of stevia outweigh its potential benefits. The organization claims that people who consume stevia are at risk for cancer or other life-threatening health problems. As a result, the public health organization has recommended that the FDA recognize the dangers of stevia and ban it for human consumption.

Which of the following, if true, most seriously undermines the public health organization's claim that stevia is dangerous?

(A) The head of the largest artificial sweetener manufacturer in the country has financed the studies exploring the health dangers of stevia.
(B) It is common knowledge that stevia is widely used in Japan, and no negative side effects have been reported.
(C) The head of the public health organization is currently on the short list for a senior position in the FDA.
(D) A large national diabetes association has publicly supported stevia as a safe sugar alternative for diabetics.
(E) No tests conducted by the public health organization indicate that stevia has ever caused cancer or any other health problems in human beings.

- 92 -

4. Conservative voter: Universal healthcare is a very controversial issue in our country that conservative voters have traditionally opposed, because of the cost to the taxpayer. Conservative voters should support universal healthcare, however, because under such a healthcare system the government would actually spend fewer tax dollars than at present. In other countries with universal healthcare, the governments spend less tax money per patient than our government currently spends for a healthcare system that is not universal.

    A weakness in this argument lies in the fact that the voter

    (A) gives an inconsistent definition of universal health care
    (B) assumes that universalizing is the only way to reduce the cost per person
    (C) changes the subject in order to establish a conclusion
    (D) relies on a partisan position to make a policy recommendation
    (E) couches an ad hominem (or personal) insult in constructive criticism

5. Language development specialists have discovered that most children learn languages best before puberty. During the years leading up to puberty, children's brains are capable of absorbing new languages with less effort than the brains of children who are post-pubescent. As a result, pre-pubescent children are able to think in a new language far more quickly than their post-pubescent counterparts, and children prior to puberty are also able to retain those languages more easily than if they learn the languages after puberty. Funding is limited for second language programs, so schools in this country tend to delay the study of modern languages until high school; but young children would benefit from second language programs in the elementary years.

    Which of the following best summarizes the main point of the passage?

    (A) Children learn languages best before puberty because their brains absorb new languages more easily than the brains of those who are post-pubescent.
    (B) There is currently not enough government funding to provide for second language programs at the elementary level.
    (C) Because of a difference in brain development, children before puberty can learn to think in a new language more quickly than children after puberty.
    (D) It is a mistake to delay the teaching of second languages until high school, as there is little chance that students will be able to retain a second language.
    (E) Because children learn languages more easily before puberty, schools should adopt second language programs at the elementary level.

Section II

Cluster 1:

A lunch line at a school has a number of different options as the students progress from station to station:

Station 1, Buns
Multigrain, White

Station 2, Meat
Turkey, Beef, Chicken

Station 3, Toppings
Lettuce, Tomatoes, Onions, Cheese, Pickles

The following rules must be followed by every child going through the lunch line:
- One bun, one meat, and three toppings must be chosen.
- If Lettuce is chosen, then Pickles will also be chosen.
- Pickles will not be chosen as a topping on a White bun.
- If Beef is chosen as a meat, then Onions may not be chosen as a topping.
- Every burger must include 3 of the five healthy options – Multigrain, Turkey, Lettuce, Tomatoes, and Onion.

1. How many valid topping combinations can go on a Multigrain and Chicken burger?

    (A) 1
    (B) 2
    (C) 3
    (D) 4
    (E) 5

2. If Beef is chosen as the meat, what is a complete list of toppings that could be chosen?

    (A) Tomatoes, Onions, Cheese
    (B) Lettuce, Tomatoes, Cheese
    (C) Lettuce, Tomatoes, Pickles
    (D) Lettuce, Onions, Pickles
    (E) Tomatoes, Pickles, Cheese

3. If a burger has Pickles, Cheese, and Turkey which of the following can be the two remaining options?

   (A) Tomatoes and White
   (B) Tomatoes and Onions
   (C) Lettuce and White
   (D) Lettuce and Beef
   (E) Lettuce and Multigrain

Cluster 2:

A security company employs six guards – A, B, C, D, E, F – to guard a chemical plant. Each guard can either be on duty or off duty, but at least one guard must be on duty at any given time.

- If A is on duty, then neither B nor C is on duty.
- D and E cannot be on duty at the same time.
- F can only be on duty if A is also on duty.
- If C is on duty, then D is also on duty.

4. What is the maximum number of guards who can be on duty at the same time?

   (A) 1
   (B) 2
   (C) 3
   (D) 4
   (E) 5

5. If A and D are both off duty, which one of the following a complete and accurate list of the other guards who could be on duty?

   (A) B
   (B) B and E
   (C) B and C
   (D) B, C, and F
   (E) B, C, E, and F

Section III

Directions: Each passage in this section is followed by a group of questions to be answered on the basis of what is <u>stated</u> or <u>implied</u> in the passage. Some questions may have more than one possible answer. However, you are to choose the <u>best</u> answer, that is, the response that most accurately and completely answers the questions, and blacken the corresponding space on your answer sheet.

English language scholars generally agree that the modern English language developed from several sources: the Anglo-Saxon language, or Old English, spoken by the Germanic peoples who migrated to the island of Britain in the fifth century; the Old Norse influences of the Vikings and the Danish kings of England in the ninth and tenth centuries; the French

5 influence of the Norman invaders in the eleventh century; and the Latin influences of the earlier Roman inhabitants and the Catholic Church. However, one mystery remains. When the Anglo-Saxons arrived in Britain, there were numerous Celtic inhabitants dwelling alongside what remained of the Roman population. Why, then, did the Anglo-Saxons, and thus the English, not absorb *more* of the Celtic languages? The English language ultimately

10 adopted very few Celtic words, so few in fact that scholars are at a loss to explain the reason with any certainty. One thing is certain: the Celtic languages are in no way related to Anglo-Saxon, indeed developing from an entirely different family of languages, so there is no question that the Anglo-Saxons did not adopt Celtic words simply because they already had very similar words of their own. So, what happened? Some scholars have suggested that the

15 Anglo-Saxons already had enough words of their own and thus did not need to borrow from the Celts, even upon arriving in a new place. For instance, if the day-to-day elements of life in Britain were similar enough to those in the Anglo-Saxon homeland, the Anglo-Saxons would not feel the need to make use of foreign words to describe their new life. This theory, however, is inconsistent with evidence that the Anglo-Saxons borrowed everyday words

20 from other languages such as Old Norse and French. Other scholars have suggested the theory that the Anglo-Saxons chose to avoid the Celtic words because the Celts were essentially a conquered people – an explanation that is strongly supported by the rapid disappearance of Celts from south and central England and their subsequent movement north and west into what would become Cornwall, Wales, and Scotland.

25

Leading linguistic scholar David Crystal disagrees with this latter hypothesis, however. He points out that among the Anglo-Saxons it was not uncommon to find children with Welsh names. The great Christian poet Cædmon and Cædwalla, the king of Wessex in the seventh century, were both noteworthy and highly respected Anglo-Saxons who bore Welsh names.

30 From a purely practical perspective, it is unlikely that Anglo-Saxon parents would bestow Celtic names on their children if those names were closely associated with a despised language or a group of people deemed inferior. As a modern example, during World War I people in England began changing their names to avoid sounding too Germanic. Even the royal family, up to that point bearing the name Saxe-Coburg-Gotha, changed the family

35 name to Windsor due to the long connection of that name with a specifically English history. Additionally, the respected Battenburg family in England, closely connected to the monarchy, felt the need to change their name to Mountbatten, as it had a less decidedly German connotation.

40 Perhaps more significantly, David Crystal raises the possibility that the word *cross*, steeped in important religious meaning for manyEnglish speakers, came from a Celtic background.

In Latin, the word is *crux*, and the Scandinavians rendered it *kross*. But there is, on the whole, very little linguistic influence on early English religious terminology from the Germanic languages or the Germanic peoples, who were decidedly pagan upon their arrival
45   to England. On the other hand, the Irish Celts were enthusiastic and thorough in their missionary efforts to England and other parts of Europe, and they rendered the Latin *crux* as *cros* in Old Irish and as *croes* in Welsh. It is highly possible that the English word *cross* and the Old Norse word *kross* were influenced by the Irish missionary work. It is unlikely that the mystery of the missing Celtic words will ever be solved satisfactorily, but what little
50   evidence remains suggests that the mystery can no longer be written off as a case of a conquered people becoming linguistically obsolete.

1.   Which of the following best states the main idea of the passage?

    (A)   Although linguistic scholars do not know why the English language has so few Celtic words, it can no longer be assumed that the Anglo-Saxons avoided Celtic words in the belief that the Celts were inferior.
    (B)   The possible Celtic derivation of the word *cross* suggests that the Anglo-Saxons interacted more closely with the Celts than was previously thought.
    (C)   New evidence suggests that the traditional belief about the Anglo-Saxon, Old Norse, French, and Latin influences on the English language is erroneous and misleading.
    (D)   The actions taken by the English during World War I indicate strongly that their forebears eradicated Celtic words for similar reasons.
    (E)   The appearance of Welsh names among significant Anglo-Saxon figures indicates that of all the Celtic peoples, the Welsh had the greatest linguistic impact on Anglo-Saxon daily life.

2.   The use of the word *connotation* in line 38 most closely suggests which of the following?

    (A)   Clear relationship
    (B)   Linguistic origin
    (C)   Theoretical definition
    (D)   Potential association
    (E)   Emotional correlation

3.   The author provides examples of English behavior toward German last names during World War I in order to do which of the following?

    (A)   Prove definitely that human nature does not change
    (B)   Undermine the theory of the Welsh influence on English names
    (C)   Use a fairly recent event to provide context for a hypothesis
    (D)   Show that the English changed names because they considered Germans inferior
    (E)   Suggest that many of the so-called "English" names are really German

4. Which of the following best describes the author's attitude toward the theory that there are few Celtic words in the English language because the Celts migrated and had no contact with the Anglo-Saxons?

    (A) Self-righteous insistence
    (B) Scholarly disagreement
    (C) Patronizing disapproval
    (D) Justifiable concern
    (E) Vitriolic dissent

5. The passage suggests that the author would probably agree with which one of the following?

    (A) There is less Latin and Old Norse influence on the English language that there is Celtic influence.
    (B) Although there seem to be few Celtic words within the English language, these words suggest a significant linguistic role.
    (C) The possible Celtic derivation of the English word *cross* alone suggests that the English viewed the Celts favorably.
    (D) The Anglo-Saxons did not adopt many Celtic words because they had enough everyday words in their own language.
    (E) Because some of the Anglo-Saxons gave their children Welsh names, the Anglo-Saxon people unquestionably had a high opinion of the Celts.

Section IV

<u>Directions:</u> The questions in this section are based on the reasoning given in brief statements or passages. It is possible that for some questions there is more than one answer. However, you are to choose the *best* answer; that is, the response that most accurately and completely answers the question. You should not make assumptions that are by commonsense standards implausible, superfluous, or incompatible with the passage. After you have chosen the best answer, blacken the corresponding space on your answer sheet.

1. An IT company is planning to open a new office in the large industrial city of Nizhny Novgorod, Russia. The IT industry has, in recent years, become one of the most important industries in Nizhny Novgorod and provides the majority of high-paying jobs for residents. At the same time, the city is currently undergoing a minor economic downturn, and a number of its residents are out of work. Additionally, the IT industry has been struggling to remain strong in Nizhny Novgorod, and many of the original IT businesses, which have traditionally been the city's most successful businesses, are failing. The IT company that plans to open a new office, however, is confident it will be highly successful.

    Given the passage above, which of the following best explains the discrepancy between the current economic situation in Nizhny Novgorod and the IT company's confidence in its likely success?

    (A) The IT company, unlike most of the original IT companies, is at the cutting edge of the IT industry and can keep its costs low.
    (B) The IT company is acquiring the building of a failed IT company, so it will not have to spend funds to build a new office.
    (C) The IT company is expected to bring much-needed jobs to Nizhny Novgorod, and many residents are excited about the new office.
    (D) The IT company is not opening the new office within Nizhny Novgorod, instead locating the office where there is less industrial scenery.
    (E) The IT company has had to take out considerable loans for the construction and maintenance of the office building.

2. Philatelist: The Swedish Treskilling Yellow is the rarest stamp in the world. It was issued in 1855, when Sweden first began issuing postage stamps. The Treskilling, or three-skilling, stamp was originally intended to be printed in blue, but was accidentally printed in yellow, the color reserved for the eight-skilling stamp. A number of Treskilling Yellow stamps were printed before the mistake was noticed in 1858. A stamp collector located the first Treskilling Yellow and sold it to another collector. Soon, it became apparent that this particular stamp might be the only remaining variety of the mistaken coloration, and the Treskilling Yellow became a desired item among stamp collectors. In 1996, it was sold for $2.06 million, making it the costliest stamp in the world. Therefore, the Treskilling Yellow is also the most valuable stamp in the world.

Which of the following statements represents the assumption on which the philatelist's conclusion depends?

(A) If another Treskilling Yellow stamp happens to be found, it will bring in a price as high as that of the current Treskilling Yellow stamp.
(B) It is the unique quality of having been printed in error that makes the Treskilling Yellow stamp as rare and valuable as it is.
(C) Because the Treskilling Yellow stamp is the only one of its kind, it would be worthless if another such stamp were located.
(D) Because the Treskilling Yellow is the only one of its kind and has currently sold for the highest price among stamp collectors, it must have the most intrinsic value.
(E) Most of the finest and costliest stamps in the world have originated from printing errors in Sweden.

Questions 3 and 4
The state of Hawaii plans to build a nuclear power plant in a town along the leeward coast of Oahu. The nuclear power plant is expected to provide new jobs for people in Oahu. The town in which the power plant will be located, however, is unhappy with the plan. A spokesperson for the town reveals to the local news station that the residents are concerned about the dangers of nuclear power, as well as the potential for another accident of the magnitude of the Chernobyl disaster. As the spokesperson notes, Chernobyl was the nuclear power plant in Ukraine where a reactor exploded in 1986, creating extremely unsafe levels of radiation for residents throughout Ukraine and parts of Eastern Europe. The long-term effects of the Chernobyl explosion included permanent health damage for many residents and a variety of birth defects among children. These possible consequences are what the Hawaiian town residents most fear, in the event that a nuclear facility in Hawaii suffers a similar accident.

3. Which of the following most undermines the spokesperson's primary argument?

(A) The nuclear fallout that occurred at Chernobyl was a one-time historical event, and it cannot be assumed a similar event would occur in Hawaii.
(B) The spokesperson is a paid member of an anti-nuclear power organization that frequently lobbies against the building of new nuclear power plants in the U.S.
(C) The advances made in nuclear power plants since the days of Chernobyl ensure that the chance of a similar nuclear explosion is almost nonexistent.
(D) The nuclear power plant will bring high-paying jobs to the community and ensure excellent benefits for all employees.
(E) The voters of the state of Hawaii have voted overwhelmingly in support of the building of the nuclear power plant.

- 100 -

4. Which of the following statements would, if true, most seriously undermine the state's attempt to build the nuclear power plant?

    (A) The community is unsure whether the new nuclear power plant can be built within the required budget.
    (B) Many of the jobs that the nuclear power plant would bring are not higher-paying than the jobs that are currently available.
    (C) The state and federal governments are offering large tax incentives for communities that begin using nuclear power.
    (D) A local builder is planning a neighborhood near the expected site of the nuclear power plant and has already sold 75% of the lots.
    (E) Ocean water surrounding Hawaii is too warm to cool a nuclear reactor, so the plant would have to use extra energy to keep a nuclear reactor cool.

5. Colorblindness is a vision deficiency that limits the ability of the sufferer to see certain colors clearly. The condition may affect a person in varying degrees, ranging from mild colorblindness with a red or green color deficiency to complete colorblindness with no ability to distinguish any colors beside dim shades of brown. The primary cause of colorblindness is believed to be a mutation on the X chromosome. Men carry a single X chromosome, possessing an XY-chromosome makeup, while women carry two X chromosomes, thus having the potential to combat colorblindness with an extra X chromosome.

    If the passage above is true, which of the following can be inferred from it?

    (A) Colorblindness is a rare condition that affects very few members of the population.
    (B) Despite the handicap, those who are colorblind might have certain advantages, particularly in seeing camouflage.
    (C) Women alone are capable of passing on a gene for colorblindness.
    (D) Because of the way colorblindness affects the X chromosome, men are more likely to be colorblind than women.
    (E) Colorblindness is entirely inherited and can be tested and identified at birth.

Writing Sample Topic

Isobel McGavin has been serving in the U.S. Army Corps of Engineers for the past ten years but is looking to transition out of the military and into a civilian position. She has used a placement company to help her find a job in the oil and gas industry, and two different oil and gas companies have offered her a senior position. Write an argument for her taking one job over the other based on the following criteria:

- Isobel wants to be able to use the knowledge she has gained as an Army engineer by applying it to cutting-edge technology in the oil and gas industry.
- Isobel wants a position that allows her to set her own goals for success and challenge herself on a daily basis.

The first company is an established leader in the oil and gas industry. The company has a history of hiring former military personnel due to the education and experience such people receive. The company is also known for using time-honored techniques with an additional concentration on innovative technology. It is currently the largest oil and gas company in the country. Isobel would replace a long-time employee who is retiring and who is known for having broadened the company's focus and contributed to considerable growth in several sectors of the oil and gas industry.

The second job offer is for a start-up company composed of experts in the oil and gas industry. These experts are hoping to incorporate innovative ideas in industry techniques. The company's stock has risen considerably since its inception two years ago, and the oil and gas industry has responded well to the company's progressive approach to drilling and production. In fact, the company is considered to be one of the most dynamic participants in the industry. Isobel would be pioneering a position for the company, one that is expected to contribute extensively to growth and development and retain the company's progressive focus.

Answers and Explanations

Logical Reasoning, Section I

Question 1

Overview: Question 1 regards a passage about the manuscript history of medieval music, noting specifically four important facts: (1) manuscripts were expensive to produce, (2) the Catholic Church was one of the few institutions able to take on this expense, because it had both the wealth and the human resources as represented by scribes, (3) most extant music from the medieval period has been recorded on manuscripts, and (4) the majority of this music is sacred music. The passage includes the added suggestion that most popular music from that era is unknown today because very little was recorded on manuscripts.

The Correct Answer:

E   In question 1, the student is asked to select a statement that is supported by the claims made in the passage. To do this, the student must infer from what is stated directly. Based on these claims, answer choice (E) is the only one that fulfills this requirement. The passage states quite clearly, "Any medieval music not recorded on manuscripts has now been lost to history. Most of the medieval music still in existence is sacred music." If most extant medieval music is sacred music, and any music not recorded on manuscripts has been lost to history, then it follows that most popular music was not recorded on manuscripts and thus has been lost to history. It can safely be inferred from this fact that historians do not know much about popular medieval music because they have almost nothing to study. Answer choice (E) is correct.

The Incorrect Answers:

A   Answer choice (A) is incorrect because the passage does not offer an evaluative judgment on the music that is still extant, nor does it suggest anywhere that sacred music was recorded because it was the "greatest music" of the period. Historians might rightly debate this issue, but the passage does not discuss it or imply anything about it.

B   As with answer choice (A), the passage does not imply answer choice (B). The passage describes facts about the way medieval music was recorded and about what medieval music still exists, but it does not provide an answer to *why* most of the extant music from the Middle Ages is sacred music. Therefore, in no place in the passage does the author suggest that the Church recorded only medieval music because it did not value popular music. Answer (B) should be eliminated immediately.

C   While answer choice (C) might very well be true, the substance of this statement is not discussed at all in the passage and cannot be inferred from any statement made within it. Answer (C) is thus irrelevant and should be eliminated immediately.

D   The passage does indicate that the Church was not necessarily the *only* institution to have the means of affording manuscripts: "As a result, **few** were able to produce or own them, and the Catholic Church, which had literate scribes as well as considerable wealth, produced and maintained **most** manuscripts during the Middle Ages." This suggests logically that other institutions such as the aristocracy might very well have been able to produce and maintain some of the manuscripts. But nowhere does the passage discuss the contents of aristocratic households or that aristocrats might have held *large numbers* of manuscripts, so this statement cannot be inferred from the passage.

Question 2

<u>Overview:</u> Question 2 presents a scenario in which the CEO of a fast-food chain makes an announcement about upcoming revisions to the chain's menu. The company is completely overhauling its menu items so that all items offered will now be healthier. Specifically, the announcement notes that the company will be removing unhealthy fats and offering smaller portions. The question asks the student to consider which of the answer choices most undermines the effect of the CEO's announcement. To find the correct answer, it is necessary to focus on the details in the CEO's comments and on what, in particular, would call into question the validity of the CEO's remarks.

<u>The Correct Answer:</u>

A   Answer choice (A) states that although the fast-food chain is indeed making the announced changes in its menu, it is also retaining certain addictive additives that have, by implication, long been in its food. As a result, the continued inclusion of these additives calls into question the company's actual commitment to offering healthy foods and raises questions about the claim that the company's food will be a healthier option than that offered by other fast-food chains. Therefore, choice (A) most seriously undermines the CEO's statements.

<u>The Incorrect Answers:</u>

B   That the CEO is receiving a large bonus is potentially suspicious, but it does not by itself undermine the CEO's claim about providing healthier food options. In other words, nothing about the bonus suggests that the menu will not in fact offer healthier items than before; answer choice (B) does not address evidence for or against the CEO's. There is no reason to be surprised that the company is rewarding the CEO in advance for a plan that will benefit the company. Thus, answer choice (B) is incorrect.

C   The response of the focus group calls into question the way that customers will respond to the food, but it does not call into question the CEO's comments about the healthy qualities of the food. Thus, answer choice (C) may be eliminated immediately.

D   While the merits of advertising to young children might be arguable, the ads themselves seem to support the company's claim that it is offering healthier choices by encouraging children to request the better menu items when they visit the fast-food chains. As a result, this answer choice seems to bring some validity to the CEO's claims of a commitment to better health, and it is incorrect.

E   The CEO makes no claim to having removed all items from the old menu. Instead, he claims that the ingredients have been improved and the menu revised. Answer choice (E) does more to support the CEO's claims than it does to undermine it, so it is incorrect.

Question 3

Overview: In Question 3, a large public health organization has recommended the banning of the herbal sweetener stevia on the grounds that stevia poses cancer risks, among other health concerns. The public health organization specifically requests that the FDA acknowledge the dangers and ban the sweetener for human consumption. The student is asked to select an answer choice that most undermines the public health organization's claim about the dangers of stevia.

The Correct Answer:

E   Answer choice (E) claims that the public health organization has no tests to back up its claims about the dangers of the sweetener. If studies have shown no correlation between consumption of stevia and incidence of cancer or other health problems, this suggests that the public health organization has no evidence to support its claim that stevia is dangerous. Therefore, answer choice (E) most undermines the organization's argument.

The Incorrect Answers:

A   Although the fact that the studies were funded by the head of the largest manufacturer of artificial sweetener raises questions about a conflict of interests, this in itself does not directly undermine the claims of the public health organization. That is, an apparent conflict of interest does not necessarily mean that the public health organization offers biased or unreliable results. Therefore, answer choice (A) cannot be the best answer.

B   The use of stevia in Japan without reported negative side effects is interesting, but it does not prove that stevia is not dangerous. This answer choice does not suggest that formal studies, for example, indicate that there is no correlation between consumption of stevia and incidence of cancer or other health problems. Mere common knowledge that stevia is used commonly in Japan does not imply that stevia is safe. Answer choice (B) is incorrect.

C   Once more, this answer choice raises a question about a conflict of interests – is the head of the public health organization trying to get a job in the FDA by providing an important health warning and thus indicating his usefulness to the FDA? Perhaps. But the passage does not indicate this in any way, nor would this motivation necessarily mean that the organization's claims are incorrect or unreliable. Answer choice (C) does not clearly undermine the organization's claims and is therefore incorrect.

D   The endorsement of a large diabetic association indicates that some believe in the health value of stevia, but this does not undermine the claims of the public health organization. As there is no indication that the diabetes association has conducted studies illustrating that stevia is safe, for example, the endorsement of stevia by the diabetes association is irrelevant to the public health organization's argument. Answer choice (D) can be eliminated at once.

Question 4

<u>Overview:</u> In question 4, a conservative voter comments on a policy traditionally opposed by conservative voters in an attempt to prove to fellow conservatives that the policy is worth supporting. Specifically, the conservative voter argues that universal healthcare is not as costly to taxpayers as other conservative voters usually believe and that the government should universalize health care because it would thereby actually spend less money per person than it currently spends. The student is asked to locate a weakness in the voter's argument.

<u>The Correct Answer:</u>

B   The weakness in the voter's argument rests on the fact that the voter seems to assume that the only way to reduce the cost of health care per person is to universalize health care (the voter argues for universal health care strictly on the grounds that it would save money relative to the current health care system). But there might be other options for reducing the cost of health care per person without universalizing health care. Answer choice (B) is most correct because it accurately states this problem.

<u>The Incorrect Answers:</u>

A   Answer choice (A) is incorrect because the voter does not explicitly define what he means by universal health care. Because he does not define what it would mean for health care to be universal in the first place, he does not offer an inconsistent definition of universal health care. Therefore, answer choice (A) cannot be correct.

C   The conservative voter does not change the subject; the voter begins with the subject of health care (relating the issue directly to traditional conservatives and the cost of health care) and stays with this subject, making a specific recommendation about that same subject at the end. Answer choice (C) cannot be correct.

D   Far from relying on a partisan position, the conservative voter rejects his usual partisan position in order to encourage other conservatives to support something that is not traditionally a part of the conservative platform. Therefore, answer choice (D) is incorrect.

E   An *ad hominem* attack is a personal attack, and there is no indication of any personal insults in the conservative voter's argument. Therefore, answer choice (E) can be eliminated immediately.

Question 5

<u>Overview:</u> Question 5 asks the student to consider an argument about language development in children before puberty and to summarize the main point of the passage. Specifically, the passage begins by pointing out that specialists in language development know that pre-pubescent children learn languages better than post-pubescent children, as the brains of pre-pubescent children are more adapted to absorbing languages. The passage then points out that funding is generally limited for incorporating second language lessons to elementary children, so schools tend to delay the learning of second languages until high school, or after puberty. In order to discern the main point, the student must consider the purpose of these details, sorting out primary details and secondary details, and consider them in the context of the argument in the passage.. It is important to remember that the student is not necessarily being asked to restate the argument itself (that

schools should teach second languages to pre-pubescent children), but to summarize the entire point of the passage in the context of the argument.

The Correct Answer:

E   Answer choice (E) best combines all of the primary elements within the context of the argument to arrive at a main point: that because of children's ability to absorb new languages before puberty, schools should adopt second language lessons for elementary-age children. Therefore, answer choice (E) is most correct.

The Incorrect Answers:

A   Answer choice (A) summarizes the point of the details in the passage but does not place these details in the context of the argument being presented. The fact that children learn languages best before puberty is significant, but it needs to be placed alongside the argument about the importance of schools teaching second languages to pre-pubescent children. Answer choice (A) is incorrect, because it leaves out important elements of the passage.

B   The author of the passage does point out that there is not enough government funding for teaching second languages, but this point seems to be made within the context of *why* schools delay language classes until the high school years; it is not a primary detail. Therefore, answer choice (B) is not correct.

C   Answer choice (C) offers a secondary detail but does not place this detail within the bigger picture offered by the passage. It does not summarize the main point of the passage and can be eliminated at once.

D   Although the author of the passage does indicate clearly that children would greatly benefit from learning second languages in the elementary years, he does not pass judgment on schools that do not offer these programs. Instead, the author provides an explanation for why these programs do not exist, suggesting that such hindrances should be overcome. Answer choice (D) fails to summarize the main point of the paragraph, so it is incorrect.

Analytical Reasoning, Section II

Cluster 1:

To diagram this problem, translate the rules into symbols. For example, if lettuce is chosen, then pickles will also be chosen, translates into **L->P**. In all, the symbol translations of the conditions for this problem are:

Station #1		Station #2		Station #3	Station #3	Station #3

$$L->P$$
$$W->\sim P$$
$$B->\sim O$$

3 of the Healthy Options: Multigrain, Turkey, Lettuce, Tomatoes, and Onion

1)   D. First fill in the basic diagram with the given information.

M		C				

Due to rule #5, 3 of the healthy options, two of the remaining options must be healthy as the Multigrain bun is healthy. If Lettuce is one of the healthy options, then Pickles must be picked as well due to rule #2, L->P. The remaining option must be healthy and can be either Onions or Tomatoes, giving two possible combinations so far. If lettuce is not chosen, then both Tomatoes and Onions must be chosen to fill out the three healthy options. Either Pickles or Cheese can be chosen as the third option adding another two possible combinations. This makes a total of four possible combinations, which is answer choice D.

2)   C. This is simply a matter of seeing which answer choices violate the rules. Answer choices A and D violate rule #4, B->~O, and are incorrect. B violates rule #2, L->P, and is thus incorrect. E violates rule #5, 3 of the healthy options, as even if the multigrain bun was chosen, that would still only be two healthy options making E incorrect. Only C does not violate any rules and is the correct choice.

3)   E. First fill in the basic diagram with the given information.

		T		P	C	

Both A and C are incorrect due to rule #5, which requires 3 of the healthy options, and they only produce a total of two healthy options if chosen. B and D are incorrect as neither fits into the basic diagram violating rule #1; B would have four toppings and D would have two meats. Only E fits into the basic diagram without violating any rules and is the correct answer.

Cluster 2:

The first step is to build a flow chart. This is done by translating the conditions into symbols and then combining them into a chart. Condition #1, If A is on duty, then neither B nor C is on duty, translates to **A->~(B or C)**. Condition #2, D and E cannot be on duty at the same time, translates to **D->~E** (E->~D also works). Condition #3, F can only be on duty if A is also on duty, translates to **F->A**. Condition #4, if C is on duty, then D is also on duty, translates to **C->D**. Conditions #1 and #3 can be connected since they both have A as a factor and conditions #2 and #4 can be connected since they both have D as a factor.

$$F -> A -> \sim(B\ or\ C)$$
$$C -> D -> \sim E$$

No further connections can be made. The C in the first and second lines cannot be connected in the flow chart as one is a C and the other is a ~C, but the fact that C is influenced by both will need to be remembered while solving the problems.

4)   **C.** Based on the flowchart, looking at the situation with A both on duty and off duty will have the greatest effect. Keep in mind that the question asks for the maximum amount of guards who can be on duty at the same time, so include anyone who could be on duty in the given situation. When A is on duty, F can be on duty as well (F->A), but neither B nor C can be on duty (A->~(B or C)). If C is not on duty, then either D or E can be on duty, but not both (D->~E). So if A is on duty, A, F, and either D or E can be on duty. Now try it with A off duty again trying to maximize the number of on duty guards. If A is off duty, then F is off duty (F->A), but both B and C can be on duty (A->~(B or C)). If C is on duty, then D is on duty as well (C->D), but E is off duty (D->~E). So if A is off duty, B, C, and D are on duty. In either case, the maximum number of guards who can be on duty at the same time is 3 making C the correct answer.

5)   **B.** If A is off duty, then F must also be off duty (F->A), eliminating D and E as answer choices. If D is off duty, then C must also be off duty (C->D), eliminating C as an answer choice as well. Both B (A->~B) and E (D->~E) can be on duty with A and D off duty, making them the complete list and B the correct answer choice since A is an incomplete list.

Reading Comprehension, Section III

<u>Synopsis:</u> This passage discusses the linguistic issue of why there are not more Celtic influences in the English language. The author begins by discussing the linguistic influences that scholars already recognize and have identified – Old English (or the language of the Anglo-Saxons), Old Norse, French, and Latin – and then proceeds to explain that scholars consider the lack of Celtic words to be a mystery. When the Anglo-Saxons arrived in Britain, a considerable population of Celts lived there already. Yet there are very few Celtic words in the English language, leading scholars to wonder why the Celts appeared to make no linguistic impact on the Anglo-Saxons. The author notes that scholars have offered several theories. Some argue that the Anglo-Saxons did not need the Celtic words, because they had enough of their own; a problem with this view is that the Anglo-Saxons borrowed plenty of words from other languages. Some scholars have suggested, then, that the Anglo-Saxons viewed the Celts as inferior people and thus avoided their language. The fact that the Celts ultimately migrated north and west – away from the Anglo-Saxons – seems to support this theory. In the second paragraph, the author considers this theory and raises questions about it, citing linguistic scholar David Crystal, who points out that there is considerable evidence that the Anglo-Saxons gave their children Welsh (or Celtic) names. For example, there is a record of an Anglo-Saxon king and a renowned religious poet bearing Welsh names. It is unlikely that the Anglo-Saxons would deliberately choose names from the language of a group of people believed to be inferior, so Crystal points out that this theory does not bear up under scrutiny. In the third paragraph, the author again cites Crystal with his suggestion that the English word *cross* might derive from Celtic sources. Again, it is unlikely that the Anglo-Saxons would adopt a word with such religious significance from a despised language. The author concludes by noting that the mystery of why there are so few Celtic words in the English language might never be solved, but that the theory that the Anglo-Saxons ignored Celtic words because the Celts were viewed as inferior ultimately does not have much historical or linguistic support.

Question 1

<u>Overview:</u> Question 1 asks the student to consider the main idea of the passage. This question does not ask for any inferences, so the student just needs to consider the author's argument and summarize it. Each paragraph contains a topic, and these topics ultimately contribute to a primary point. What the student needs to watch for in the answer choices are options that mention a supporting idea but that do not reflect the main point of the passage. The correct answer choice must encompass the evidence in the passage with a single statement.

<u>The Correct Answer:</u>

A   Although the first paragraph seems to provide a great deal of information about the background of the English language, as well as theories about the lack of Celtic words, it is the final sentence of the first paragraph and the first sentence of the second paragraph that indicate the direction the passage will be taking. The author notes that one theory in particular seems to have support, but then goes on to say that a leading linguistic scholar disagrees with it. The rest of the passage explains Crystal's evidence that weakens the initial theory, and the final sentence of the third paragraph provides the main point: "It is unlikely that the mystery of the missing Celtic words will ever be solved satisfactorily, but what little evidence remains suggests that the mystery can no longer be written off as a case of a conquered people becoming linguistically obsolete." Answer choice (A) most closely summarizes this, so it is the correct answer.

The Incorrect Answers:

B   Answer choice (B) is incorrect, because it focuses on a supporting piece of evidence Crystal has provided to undermine a theory, but that is not, in itself, the main point of the passage. Answer choice (B) is incorrect.

C   Although the author does suggest that there might be considerable significance to the few Celtic words that are in the English language, the author does *not* claim or suggest anywhere that these words render other linguistic sources less significant. Additionally, the author does not indicate that there is any evidence contradicting the traditionally recognized influences. Answer choice (C) is clearly incorrect.

D, E   As in answer choice (B), the example of the English changing German names during World War I, as well as the example of the occurrence of Welsh names among the Anglo-Saxons, is intended to give supporting evidence; such examples are not meant to represent the primary argument. In addition, answer choice (E) states, "of all the Celtic peoples the Welsh had the greatest linguistic impact on Anglo-Saxon daily life," an idea unsupported by the passage. Answer choices (D) and (E) are incorrect.

Question 2

Overview: In question 2, the student is asked to select a synonymous phrase for a word that is used in the passage. The student will need to consider the word itself, with its dictionary definitions, and then place the word within the context of the sentence and consider how it is being used. (If the student does not know the meaning of the word, the student should infer what basic idea is intended by considering the context in which the word appears.) In question 9, the word in question is *connotation*, which is defined as a connection, association, or secondary meaning. In the passage, the word is being used to convey the English concern that their names were connected to German names or assumed to be German. With this in mind, the student needs to consider the answer choices.

The Correct Answer:

D   Of all the answer choices, answer choice (D) best conveys the idea of "connection" and "assumption" with the phrase *potential association*. As the passage notes, the English changed their names "to avoid sounding too Germanic." In other words, they feared the potential for their names being associated with German names. Answer choice (D), therefore, is correct.

The Incorrect Answers:

A   Answer choice (A) offers a good option, but the passage does not suggest that the English knew there would be a *clear relationship*, nor does the word *connotation* in the context of the passage suggest a clear relationship. Instead, it suggests the possibility of a connection between English names and German names, a connection that answer choice (A) does not indicate. Answer choice (A) is incorrect.

B   Although the fears of the English were about a linguistic matter (they were concerned that their names might be connected with German names), the phrase *linguistic origin* cannot replace the word *connotation* in meaning. Answer choice (B) is incorrect.

C   Although the word *connotation* can, in some cases, indicate a definition that is more theoretical than it is concrete, there is nothing in the use of the word *connotation* in the passage to suggest that the English were concerned about a *theoretical definition*. Answer choice (C) is incorrect.

E   Although the decision by some English people to change their names might have been based on emotion, the passage does not suggest this. Because there is no clear suggestion of emotion in the passage, answer choice (E) is incorrect.

Question 3

<u>Overview:</u> Question 3 asks the student to consider the role of the example about English actions toward German names during World War I. And as with the discussion of the word *cross*, this particular information offers secondary details that support the main point of the passage. The student needs to consider the English/German names discussion, then, within the context of the main point, as well as within the context of the statements immediately around it. The correct answer might or might not mention specifically the main point of the passage, but it will show that the example fits well with that main point.

<u>The Correct Answer:</u>

C   The discussion of the English decision to change German or German-sounding names during World War I follows a paraphrased reference from David Crystal about the fact that the Anglo-Saxons would probably not have given their children Welsh names if those names were associated with something or someone negative. Since there is no immediate connection to Welsh names and German names, the student can assume that the author is intending to use this particular example to show how perceptions of peoples (whether they are Germans or Celts) influence the use of names associated with those peoples. Answer choice (C) expresses this idea and is thus the correct answer.

<u>The Incorrect Answers:</u>

A   The passage makes no reference to human nature, and although it might be thought that associating names from certain linguistic backgrounds with either positive or negative qualities is a facet of human nature, there is not enough information in the passage to support this point. More specifically, the question of human nature is not related to the larger question of the impact of certain Celtic words in the English language. Therefore, answer choice (A) cannot be correct.

B   If the discussion of the English response to German names were being used to support the traditional theory about Anglo-Saxons viewing the Celts as inferior, this argument might indeed undermine the theory of Welsh influence. But in the context of the second paragraph, it actually supports the point about Anglo-Saxons embracing certain Welsh influences, because it indicates clearly that the Anglo-Saxons did *not* avoid Welsh names. Answer choice (B) is incorrect.

D   Answer choice (D) seems briefly promising, because the example of the English immediately follows this statement by the author: "it is unlikely that Anglo-Saxon parents would bestow Celtic names on their children if those names were closely associated with a despised language or a group of people deemed inferior." This seems to suggest that if the English during World War I did to the Germans what the much earlier Anglo-Saxons did *not* do to the Welsh, then the English might have viewed the Germans as inferior. But once again, this is not the main point of the passage. Answer choice (D) is thus incorrect.

E   The passage does not indicate at any point that English names might really be German. In fact, it seems to suggest just the opposite – that if many of the English changed German names, the names are now English. More to the point, however, this inference does not have a strong connection to the main point of the passage, and therefore answer choice (E) is incorrect.

Question 4

Overview: Question 4 asks the student to consider the author's tone toward the traditional argument that the Anglo-Saxons might have deliberately avoided Celtic words because they viewed the Celts as inferior. Certain key words in the passage will help discern whether the author's tone is one of vitriolic disagreement, patronization, or something else altogether. Such phrases include "Other scholars have **suggested the theory**...," "leading linguistic scholar David Crystal **disagrees**...," "the mystery **can no longer be written off**..." All of these turns of phrase suggest a polite scholarly discussion in which one scholar (the author) disagrees with other scholars – firmly but not necessarily rudely. The student should select an answer choice that best reflects this.

The Correct Answer:

B   Answer choice (B) is the only answer choice to present the best description of the author's tone: *scholarly disagreement*. The author is polite but holds to a certain view and defends that view. Answer choice (B), therefore, is correct.

The Incorrect Answers:

A   The author might hold firmly to an opinion, but there is no tone of *insistence*, nor is the author *self-righteous* at any point. Answer choice (A) is clearly incorrect.

C   The author clearly disagrees with the traditional viewpoint, but disagreement alone does not guarantee a patronizing attitude; and this passage does not suggest a patronizing tone at any point. Had the author mentioned the differing viewpoint repeatedly in order to belittle those who held it, the tone might be described as patronizing. As it is, however, the author mentions the viewpoint only twice and the scholars holding the view once, allowing the rest of the discussion to focus on evidence that supports his own perspective.

D   The author's concern about the traditional viewpoint might be justifiable in his own mind, but the passage does not necessarily convey this tone. Instead, the tone is a scholarly one that leaves emotion at the door and relies on evidence. Answer choice (D) is incorrect.

E   Although the author does disagree with the traditional viewpoint, there is nothing in the passage to indicate vitriol. Answer choice (E) can be eliminated immediately.

Question 5

<u>Overview:</u> Question 5 asks with which answer choice the author would likely agree. As with all questions like this, the student needs to consider what is stated directly in the passage and what can be inferred from these statements. The student should also take such qualities as tone into account.

<u>The Correct Answer:</u>

B   The author notes in the first paragraph that there are few Celtic words in the English language and then implies in the second and third paragraphs that *although* there are few words, these words suggest a significant linguistic role (significant because the word *cross* itself, for example, has religious significance). Answer choice (B), therefore, is correct.

<u>The Incorrect Answers:</u>

A   Although the author suggests that *one word* in the English language might have a Celtic origin as opposed to an Old Norse origin, it cannot be inferred that the author believes there are more words (in English) of Celtic origin than of Latin or Old Norse origin. In fact, the author states several times that there are not many Celtic words in the English language, so the passage does not support the inference that one word is indicative of a much broader trend. Answer choice (A) is incorrect.

C   The author uses the example of the word *cross* to indicate the potential for significant Celtic influences on English. Although this is related to the issue of how the English viewed the Celts (favorably or unfavorably), the passage does not indicate that the author believes that the origin of the word *cross* alone signifies how the English viewed the Celts. The author also cites David Crystal's mention of the Welsh names; so, it cannot be inferred that the author believes that *cross* alone is significant in regard to the isssue of how the English viewed the Celts. Answer choice (C) is incorrect.

D   The author cites the information in answer choice (D) as one reason why some scholars believe that Anglo-Saxons did not absorb many Celtic words. However, the author also points out that this theory "is inconsistent with evidence that the Anglo-Saxons borrowed everyday words from other languages such as Old Norse and French." Answer choice (D) must be incorrect.

E   The author notes that it is unlikely that the Anglo-Saxons would have given their children Welsh names if they believed the Celts to be inferior, but it cannot necessarily be inferred from this alone that the Anglo-Saxons *unquestionably* had a high opinion of all Celts. This strong claim goes well beyond anything stated or implied in the passage. Answer choice (E) is incorrect.

Logical Reasoning, Section IV

Question 1

Overview: Question 1 describes a situation in which an IT company is planning to open a new office in the city of Nizhny Novgorod, Russia, where IT is a major industry. The passage notes, however, that the economy has been in a state of weakness and that many residents are out of work. The IT industry is also weak, and a number of IT businesses that have been in the city for some time are now closing. However, the company opening the new office is confident of its success. The question asks the student to consider an explanation for why this is. To select the correct answer, the student needs to consider the details in the passage, reflecting what might set the one IT company above the rest, even during an economic downturn.

The Correct Answer:

A   Answer choice (A) is the only answer choice that provides a sufficient explanation for why the IT company can be so confident of its success in spite of a struggling economy: its technology is up to date (and thus will be in demand), and it is able to keep its costs low (thus offsetting the economic weakness). Answer choice (A) also notes that the other IT businesses in Nizhny Novgorod have not kept their technology up to date, so this places the company with the new office at a distinct competitive advantage. Answer choice (A) is the correct answer.

The Incorrect Answers:

B   Although purchasing an existing building instead of building a new one creates an immediate financial advantage, it does not explain why the IT company with the new office can succeed where its competitors cannot. Answer choice (B) is incorrect due to insufficient details to explain the discrepancy.

C   The employment opportunities offered by the IT company with the new office has some potential to explain its expected success. However, it is not clear from the answer choice *how* the company will pay new hires, that is, how the company can afford new hires. This answer choice alone does not provide a sufficient reason for the company's confidence in its financial success. Answer choice (C) cannot be correct.

D   The presence of industrial scenery does not clearly contribute to a lack of business success, so answer choice (D) does not explain why the IT company with the new office can be confident of its success. Were the answer choice to include some information about *why* the industrial scenery has hurt other IT businesses and *how* it has added to their failure, this might be a good possibility. As it is, though, answer choice (D) cannot be correct.

E   Far from explaining the reason for the IT company's confidence, answer choice (E) raises questions about the potential for its success by claiming that the company will immediately have large debts to pay off. Answer choice (E) is not correct and can be eliminated immediately.

Question 2

Overview: Question 2 presents a statement from a philatelist (a stamp collector) who is discussing a very rare stamp, "the rarest stamp in the world," according to the philatelist: the Swedish Treskilling Yellow. The philatelist notes that the stamp is so rare because it was originally printed in error and only one remains. As of 1996, the Treskilling Yellow was sold for $2.06 million dollars and is now the most expensive stamp in the world. The philatelist concludes that it is thus the most valuable stamp in the world. The student must consider which of the answer choices represents the assumption on which the philatelist's conclusion depends. The first factor to consider is the conclusion itself – that the Treskilling Yellow is the most valuable stamp in the world. The second factor is the detail that supports the conclusion: (1) that the stamp is the only one of its kind to have been found, and (2) that it has sold for the highest price. According to the statements made by the philatelist these details make the stamp the most valuable in the world, so the correct answer choice will reflect this.

The Correct Answer:

D   Answer choice (D) best summarizes the details noted in the Overview – that the philatelist consider the stamp to be the most valuable because it is unique and because it has sold for the most money. Therefore, answer choice (D) is correct.

The Incorrect Answers:

A   The information in the passage suggests that the philatelist's belief in the stamp's value is based in part on the fact that there is only one stamp known to be in existence. Therefore, answer choice (A) cannot be correct, because the philatelist's comments cannot be said to assume that a second stamp would sell for as much.

B   Answer choice (B) is partially correct insofar as it expresses some of the information that supports the philatelist's claim: the original error that printed the stamp in a different color has contributed to its rarity and its desirability among stamp collectors. However, this is a supporting detail and does not necessarily indicate the primary assumptions on which the philatelist's argument depends. Answer choice (B) is not correct.

C   Answer choice (C) offers a contrary assumption to answer choice (A): that the Treskilling Yellow would actually be *worthless* if a second stamp were found. But there is nothing in the passage to suggest that the philatelist believes this, so answer choice (C) can be eliminated due to insufficient support.

E   The assumption that "the finest and costliest stamps in the world have originated from printing errors in Sweden" is utterly insupportable based on information in the passage. The philatelist notes only that *one stamp* is the costliest in the world, and this just happens to be because it is rare and because it is the result of a printing error. There is no further information about other rare and costly stamps, so answer choice (E) can be eliminated immediately.

Questions 3 and 4

<u>Overview:</u> Questions 3 and 4 discuss plans by the state of Hawaii to build a nuclear power plant in a town on the leeward coast of Oahu. The townspeople are not happy with this plan and have acquired a spokesperson to explain their concerns about the intended facility. According to the spokesperson, the town's primary fear is that the new nuclear power plant will create another incident like the Chernobyl disaster; the spokesperson cites details of that disaster, including its long-term effects. Question 17 asks for the answer choice that most undermines the spokesperson's claims; question 18 asks for the problem that most undermines the state's plans to build the facility. To answer question 17, the student should begin by noting the main point of the spokesperson's argument: the people of the town are opposed to the building of the nuclear power plant because they fear an explosion like the one that happened at Chernobyl. To answer question 18, the student needs to consider which answer choice has the greatest effect on the state's plans by taking into account the options among the answer choices – the answer choice that provides a clear problem with the construction or running of the plant will be correct.

Question 3

<u>The Correct Answer:</u>

C   Answer choice (C) explains the problem with the spokesperson's argument. In a discussion of an event that occurred over two decades before, the spokesperson fails to consider whether technology has improved since then (particularly in light of the reasonable assumption that since the events at Chernobyl, nuclear engineers would be motivated to ensure that such an accident would not happen again). Because answer choice (C) states specifically that current nuclear power plants are designed to prevent similar accidents, answer choice (C) is correct.

<u>The Incorrect Answers:</u>

A   Answer choice (A) approaches a part of the problem in the spokesperson's argument, but it does not undermine it completely. This answer choice suggests that the fears of the people in the town are not justified, but offers only a vague claim that they *cannot be applied*. Without further information to explain *why* they cannot be applied (such as the correct answer choice provides), this is simply not enough to undermine the argument effectively. Answer choice (A), therefore, is incorrect.

B   The role of the spokesperson as a paid lobbyist against nuclear power might motivate him to speak on the town's behalf, but this does not necessarily undermine his argument in any way. If anything, it simply explains why he was hired. Answer choice (B) is incorrect.

D, E   Although answer choices (D) and (E) offer explanations for why there should be support for the intended nuclear power plant, they both fail to offer a clear statement that *undermines the argument* of the spokesperson. In fact, both answer choices (D) and (E) essentially create red herrings (that is, change the subject) by diverting the spokesperson's argument in a different direction and thus failing to address the substance of the argument. Therefore, answer choices (D) and (E) are incorrect.

Question 4

The Correct Answer:

E   Answer choice (E) indicates the most serious problem that could undermine the state's plans to build the new nuclear power plant. If the facility needs cold water to cool the reactor core, the extra energy required to cool the reactor would add extra expense to the construction and maintenance of the facility, potentially damaging its chances of being a viable energy alternative. Answer choice (E) is correct.

The Incorrect Answers:

A   The opinion of the community regarding the budget is a legitimate issue. The community's fears alone, however, do not necessarily indicate the most serious problem that could undermine the construction of the plant. Regardless of how well founded (or not) those fears are, these fears can be allayed, or the project might be proceed in spite of them. (This contrasts with the answer choice (E): if the statement this answer choice describes were true, it is very unlikely that the plant would be built.) Answer choice (A) is correct.

B   Although the value of the jobs that the plant will bring into the community is a worthwhile consideration, answer choice (B) offers too little detail to present a problem that is as serious as the problem indicated in the correct answer choice. Therefore, this answer choice is incorrect.

C   Answer choice (C) does raise questions about the connection between state officials and the managers of the nuclear power plant, but this alone does not necessarily mean that there is corruption involved. Answer choice (C) does not contain enough information to undermine the state's plans and is thus incorrect.

D   The plans of the local builder do not by themselves necessarily present a problem as serious as the problem described in the correct answer choice; again, the latter would almost certainly prevent the building of the plant, while this is not true of answer choice (D). Answer choice (D) is thus incorrect.

Question 5

Overview: Question 5 gives information about the vision deficiency known as colorblindness, wherein sufferers have varying degrees of an inability to distinguish color. The author explains that colorblindness is believed to originate from a mutation of the X chromosome. The author also states that men have an XY chromosome makeup, while women have an XX chromosome makeup. The question asks for a statement that may be inferred from the passage, based on the information contained within it.

The Correct Answer:

D   At the end of the passage, the author notes, "Men carry a single X chromosome, possessing an XY-chromosome makeup, while women carry two X chromosomes, thus having the potential to combat colorblindness with an extra X chromosome." This suggests that men are more likely to be colorblind than women because men have only a single X chromosome. Of all the answer choices, answer choice (D) can best be inferred from the passage, so it is correct.

The Incorrect Answers:

A   The author makes no comment on the population percentage of colorblindness sufferers, so it is impossible to infer safely that colorblindness is a rare condition. The student might know from prior knowledge that colorblindness *is* a fairly rare condition, but the question asks for what can be inferred from the passage, not what the student already knows to be true. As answer choice (A) cannot be inferred, it cannot be correct.

B   Again, the information contained within answer choice (B) might well be true, but it cannot be inferred from the passage. The author notes only that colorblindness "limits the ability of the sufferer to see certain colors clearly. The condition may affect a person in varying degrees, ranging from mild colorblindness with a red or green color deficiency to complete colorblindness with no ability to distinguish any colors beside dim shades of brown." This in itself does not suggest clearly that colorblindness sufferers would be able to see camouflage well, so answer choice (B) is incorrect.

C   The author does not discuss the way that colorblindness is passed on, much less the fact that colorblindness is a hereditary condition. Although the author does imply that women are less likely to be colorblind than men, the author does *not* necessarily imply that women alone pass the condition on.. Answer choice (C) cannot be inferred from the passage, so it is incorrect.

E   As with answer choice (C), the author does not discuss whether colorblindness is an inherited condition. So, it is impossible to determine from the passage if the author also believes that colorblindness can be tested at birth. Answer choice (E) infers details that are not supported by the passage, so it is incorrect.

Writing Sample Topic

How to Approach the Sample Essay

There is no right or wrong answer for the writing sample, and LSAC does not actually give the essay a score. But the law schools to which the students apply will receive a copy of the essay, so students need to shape a response that indicates their writing skills to these schools. There are several important considerations to keep in mind when developing the essay:

1. Schools want to know that students have strong communication skills, so the essay should be clear and concise and provide a solid response to the topic, with a strong development of each paragraph.
2. The essay should stay entirely on topic: students should not veer off the point by including unnecessary examples or by failing to address the primary focus of the topic. The key is to remain relevant and answer the topic question with clear exposition.
3. Essay writing establishes that a student is able to develop persuasive ideas and organize them effectively. Schools look for these skills, so the essay provides students with the opportunity to indicate an ability to make a credible and well-developed argument in written form.

FREE Study Skills DVD Offer

Dear Customer,

Thank you for your purchase from Mometrix.

As a way of showing our appreciation and to help us better serve you, we have developed a Study Skills DVD that we would like to give you for <u>FREE</u>. **This DVD covers our "best practices" for studying for your exam, from using our study materials to preparing for the day of the test.**

All that we ask is that you email us your feedback that would describe your experience so far with our product. Good, bad or indifferent, we want to know what you think!

To get your **FREE Study Skills DVD**, email <u>freedvd@mometrix.com</u> with "MY DVD" in the subject line and the following information in the body of the email:

    a.   The name of the product you purchased.

    b.   Your product rating on a scale of 1–5, with 5 being the highest rating.

    c.   Your feedback. It can be long, short, or anything in-between, just your impressions and experience so far with our product. Good feedback might include how our study material met your needs and will highlight features of the product that you found helpful.

    d.   Your full name and shipping address where you would like us to send your free DVD.

If you have any questions or concerns, please don't hesitate to contact me directly.

Thanks again!

Sincerely,
Jay Willis
Vice President
<u>jay.willis@mometrix.com</u>
1-800-673-8175

50245111R10073

Made in the USA
Middletown, DE
24 June 2019